The Classic Rovers

The Classic Rovers
1934 — 1977

A collector's guide
by James Taylor

MOTOR RACING PUBLICATIONS LTD
Unit 6, The Pilton Estate, 46 Pitlake, Croydon CR0 3RY, England

ISBN 0 900549 75 0
First published 1983
Reprinted 1989

Photosetting by Tek-Art Ltd., London SE20
Printed in Great Britain by The Amadeus Press Ltd.,
Huddersfield, West Yorkshire HD2 1YJ

Contents

Introduction

Like a number of other motor car manufacturers, Rover waited a long time before achieving greatness. Although the original company had pioneered the Starley Safety Cycle, the motorcycles and cars it produced in the first three decades of the 20th century were almost uniformly dull and uninspiring. Rover's greatness was achieved when control of the Company devolved into the hands of the Wilks brothers – Spencer Wilks, who left his position as joint Managing Director of Hillman to join Rover in 1929, and Maurice Wilks, who left Hillman to take charge of engineering and design at Rover in 1930. Maurice died in 1963, and his brother died eight years later, but their imprint on all the models discussed in this book was unmistakable.

The cars produced under the Wilks regime represent something peculiarly British in a way that perhaps no other manufacturer's products do. They were aimed fairly and squarely at the well-to-do middle classes which emerged in Britain after the Depression and, until changing world markets in the 1950s and 1960s forced some concessions to export requirements, they were marked by an insularity of approach which could fairly be said to parallel that often described as characteristic of the British people.

The Wilks formula was twofold. For the cars themselves, the brothers specified a combination of urbane good taste, refinement, reliability, longevity and imaginative engineering within a conservative appearance. For the Company, they made sure Rover would succeed by remaining small and by putting quality before quantity. Other 'middle-class' manufacturers overstepped the mark and were absorbed by the big combines, but Rover stayed happily independent until the creation of the British Leyland combine in the late 1960s forced them to capitulate by buying-out their major component suppliers. It is a measure of the esteem in which they were held that so many loyal Rover engineers were immediately appointed to top posts in the new combine. Alas, the new models planned for the 1970s never reached production, and Rover were forced into a shotgun marriage with Triumph to produce the SD1 – a brilliant machine in its own right, but almost totally unrelated to the Wilks philosophy. At the time of writing, the SD1 replacement seems likely to be a joint British Leyland-Honda production, which is certainly not in the Wilks tradition of independence.

Even though the Wilks brothers imposed on Rover an approach which was never allowed to waver, they were far from being dictators; they simply had a clear vision of what Rover should do, and in a kindly and gentlemanly way they ensured that the Company did it. Nor did they stifle innovation, though Rover's advanced engineering teams were always rather obscured by the outwardly conventional saloon cars. It is worth drawing attention to the gas turbine experiments, to the host of technically fascinating prototypes which for one reason or another have never gone into production, and above all to the phenomenally successful Land-Rover and Range Rover, as further indications of what the Wilks brothers did for Rover. There are those still working for the Company who would swear that the Wilks brothers *were* Rover; if that is so, then perhaps this book may be considered a small tribute to their achievements.

A word of explanation should be added here about Rover model designations. For many years, the problem of what constituted a P1 or P2 has been disputed, and the significance of the 'P' prefix has been hotly debated. No-one has ever doubted that the P3 was the independent-front-suspension car introduced in 1948, because the Rover Company called it that in some of their literature. Enthusiasts and historians alike have tentatively identified the P1 as the first range of new cars with underslung chassis produced under the Wilks regime, and P2s as their rebodied successors, a range which was briefly revived after the War.

The truth is rather different. It appears that wartime work on military projects first inspired the Wilks brothers to give their postwar car products code-numbers, and several senior engineers who worked at Rover in the immediate postwar period confirm that 'P' stood quite simply for 'Postwar'. Quite naturally, the revival of the prewar car was known as P1; P2 was the designation earmarked for a re-engined P1 which never went into production, and P3 followed on logically and chronologically from there. However, it is clear that the P1 and P2 designations were practically unknown outside the small circle of management and senior design engineers; as far as sales and service staff were concerned, pre-P3 cars were simply identified by their season of manufacture and horsepower rating.

Ascot, March 1983   JAMES L. TAYLOR

Acknowledgements

Dozens, possibly hundreds, of people have contributed to the pool of knowledge from which the information in this book is drawn. It is not possible to thank them all individually here, but my thanks do go to the following, who have contributed directly to the present undertaking: David Bache, Stan Banting, Gordon Bashford, Richard Beetham, Ian Elliott, Tony Holder, Geoff Kent, William Martin-Hurst, David Michie, Alan Milstead, Adrian Mitchell, Jim Ritson, Jack Swaine, Brian Terry, Chris Wickham and Philip Wilson. Special thanks are due to Glyn Jones, who kindly checked through several chapters in draft form and saved me from a number of errors and ambiguities.

In addition, I should like to express my gratitude to Anders Clausager at BL Heritage, to Harry Mills of the Rover photographic archives, and to *Autocar* and *Motor* for allowing me to quote from their Road Tests in the Appendices. Finally, I am very grateful to my editor/publisher John Blunsden for giving me the opportunity to write at such length on a favourite subject, and to my wife Lesley Ann for her forbearance and for remaining a Rover enthusiast throughout.

All photographs in this book are used by kind permission of BL Heritage, except where noted otherwise.

J.L.T.

This rather pretty 10/25 is typical of the smaller Rovers built just prior to the Wilks regime. First registered in 1930, it was photographed in 1981.

At the other end of the range were cars like this 1928 Weymann-bodied Light 6 Sports Saloon. The design was known as the *Blue Train* after an example raced the St Raphael – Calais *Blue Train* express across France in 1920 – and won. This beautifully restored example is one of the few survivors. The fabric-covered Weymann bodies deteriorated very quickly, and excessive reliance on them was one factor in Rover's downhill slide at the end of the 1920s.

CHAPTER 1

Ancestors and parentage

The revival of Rover

At the end of the 1920s, the Rover Company was in a sorry state. It had lost both its earlier reputation and a great deal of money as the result of poor management, inefficient production methods and, above all, concentration on the wrong type of cars compounded by erroneous sales forecasting. In 1928, the shareholders forced the resignation of the then Chairman and elected to the post Colonel Frank Searle. Searle was not a motor industry man himself, but he was enough of a businessman to recognize that the company would not survive without management experienced in that industry. He persuaded his Board to agree to the creation of a new post, that of General Manager. In September 1929, that post was filled by Spencer Wilks, the former joint Managing Director of Hillman.

Although Wilks undoubtedly had his own ideas about the best methods to achieve profitability, for the moment his task was to improve the existing product. The Rover Board was committed to a policy of producing small cars in large numbers and large cars in small numbers; the 1930 cars were already on sale and the 1931 models in the planning stages and, in any case, Wilks was not yet in any position to influence overall policy. For 1931, production of the small 10/25 model was to be increased, prices cut, and production of the larger models (the 2-litre/Light Six and the Meteor/Light Twenty) was to be reduced. Spencer Wilks set to with a will arranging for a new 10/25 variant, the 10 Special, to be fitted with the Pressed Steel body of the Hillman Minx; as the husband of one of William Hillman's many daughters, he was able to reach an advantageous

agreement with his former employers! Nevertheless, Rover's finances at the end of the 1931 fiscal year were in worse trouble than ever, the large number of cars remaining unsold bearing witness to the mistaken policy of trying to increase profits simply by increasing production.

Frank Searle left the UK at the end of 1931 to visit Rover's freshly-opened New Zealand factory, and Spencer Wilks took over the day-to-day running of the Company. His influence had already begun to change the face of Rover, however. A new model introduced in the autumn of 1931 at his behest was a 12hp car based on the steel-bodied 10 Special, but with the additional refinement of a six-cylinder engine. This Pilot shared with the 10 Special a number of chassis and transmission refinements which, together with the mechanical improvements introduced across the range, were evidence of the work Maurice Wilks was now putting in as Rover's Chief Design Engineer. Also scheduled for introduction in 1931 had been a tiny two-seater economy car with a rear-mounted air-cooled engine, but it never reached production. Probably the Rover Board vetoed it because of the capital investment required, but it would be nice to think that the Wilks brothers – both of whom had been involved in its development, no doubt against their better judgment – had had a hand in the demise of the Scarab, which at that time could only have spelt disaster for the Company.

At the close of the 1932 trading season, Rover's finances were still in poor health, and Lloyd's Bank insisted on nominating to the Board a Financial Director from outside the Company. The appointee was a Birmingham accountant called H.Howe Graham, and he not surprisingly turned to Rover's General Manager for assistance in feeling his way into his new job. The two men hit it off extraordinarily well; Graham was impressed by Spencer Wilks' talents, and made sure that he was appointed to the Board, placing executive power in his own and Wilks' hands. Between them, they set about reorganizing the ailing company, Graham dealing with the administrative side, while Wilks concentrated on products and manufacturing.

First, Wilks decided it was important to make proper use of available resources. Cars were being built and components being made in too many places, and so the decision was taken to sell off the under-utilized Meteor Works in Coventry's Queen Victoria Road (the original Rover factory), and to concentrate as much work as possible at Tyseley, in Birmingham, and at Helen Street, in Coventry. The former was to build engines and transmissions, while Helen Street, now named the New Meteor Works, would undertake final assembly. This plan took immediate effect from the end of 1932.

The second part of the Wilks plan involved the rationalization and improvement of the company's products. Wilks reasoned that Rover needed a range of cars based on common components, with a recognizable family identity, and quality beyond reproach. Broadly speaking, the plan to achieve this spanned six years and consisted of two major phases. The first was standardization of mechanical components and the second was that of the bodies, but throughout, the overriding priority was to be quality rather than quantity.

The 1933 season saw the start of Rover's upward trend. Howe Graham achieved enormous savings by skilful reorganization of expenditure, and the new cars bore eloquent witness to the Wilks 'quality' approach. Production figures were lower than those for 1932, partly because of limited capacity at the New Meteor Works, but more important was the evidence of satisfied customers in the company's £7,511 profit for the year; in 1931, the loss had been £80,000! Besides the improvement in quality across the range, the 1933 Rovers all featured a freewheel in the

The first signs of the Wilks influence were discernible by 1931. This photograph shows 12hp Pilots nearest the camera – note that all the bodies are now panelled in steel. Just visible on the left are two examples with the rare van body.

transmission; the Pilot was uprated from 12hp to 14hp, and there was a new chassis configuration with an underslung rear on the new high-performance Speed 14 Pilot model. In the meantime, Frank Searle had resigned as Rover's Managing Director without ever returning from his New Zealand trip and, with the inevitability of a good fairytale, Spencer Wilks had succeeded him. The stage was now set for the first of the 'Wilks Rovers'.

The Hastings Coupe

The 1933 Speed 14 Pilot was in so many ways prophetic of Rover development in the 1930s that it deserves detailed consideration here. On its introduction in the autumn of 1932, no-one could have known how much future Rovers would owe to it, although those employed at Helen Street probably knew that its new chassis configuration was planned for use on other models later. By introducing this on the Speed 14 Pilot, a model for relatively limited production, Rover both deferred the cost of wholesale

The 14hp six-cylinder engine was designed by Major B.H. Thomas who, like the Wilks brothers, was a former Hillman employee. This example was photographed in a 1934 Sports Saloon by Alan Milstead.

retooling and allowed the design to gather an aura of exclusivity which could only help sales later when it was introduced on the more mundane models.

In conception, the chassis was a typically astute move by the Wilks brothers. The Pilot's 1,577cc six-cylinder engine was given three carburettors, a high-compression cylinder head with streamlined ports and manifolding, and a 'sports' exhaust system to release a little extra power. The result was an exceptionally high output of 54bhp at 4,800rpm, which was transmitted through a four-speed gearbox to a lowered (4·8:1) rear axle ratio to give the car a maximum speed of around 80mph with acceleration to match. This in itself would have made for an attractive model, but the real

master-stroke lay in the new chassis frame. This had a wheelbase 6in longer than the standard Pilot's, together with side members which swept under rather than over the rear axle. As a result, it lent itself to the fitting of long, low sporting bodywork without the usual penalty in closed bodies of intolerably reduced rear headroom.

Besides the cycle-winged four-door Sports Saloon which Rover were wont to advertise, a range of bodies by outside coachbuilders was available, and one of the most pleasingly proportioned was a two-door close-coupled coupe with sweeping wings and an enclosed boot built by Carbodies of Coventry. An early example of the Coachbuilt Coupe won two coachwork awards in the 1933 RAC Rally, and Rover

This splendidly-preserved 1934 10hp Saloon was recorded by Alan Milstead's camera in 1982.

lost no time in capitalizing on this achievement. The Carbodies design was promoted to the status of a catalogued model under the name of Hastings Coupe, taking its title from the town where the RAC Rally had finished. It was offered on the Speed 14 and Speed 20 chassis, although in the latter model's case the absence of an underslung rear chassis led to the usual restriction in rear headroom.

Although relatively few were built (Rover production figures suggest that no more than 204 Speed 14 Pilot chassis were made in 1933), it is possible to recapture some of the impact which the Speed 14 Hastings made at the time from contemporary road-tests. Not only was the car capable of acceleration and maximum speed way above its class, but its suspension and handling allowed this performance to be put to good use without discomfort to the occupants. The

brakes, a Lockheed hydraulic system when other Rover models made do with mechanical brakes, were also well up to the performance. Allied to the qualities of the chassis was a well-finished, good-looking and comfortable body, with a number of practical features of considerable merit. 'The doors are wide', claimed a contemporary sales brochure, 'and the floor level is low allowing easy entrance to both front and rear seats.' Moreover, 'the built-in luggage compartment of the Hastings Coupe body...is considerably more commodious than is usual in a car of this type. Ample room is provided for suitcases and if required the lid of the compartment can be used as an extension.' The spare wheel was mounted externally on this lid under a neat detachable cover. The passenger compartment was lavishly equipped with pile carpets, ashtrays, hanging straps and a sun visor.

A rear view of the rare 1934 10hp Sports Saloon, this one pictured in 1981. Sports Saloons on the larger-engined chassis had a metal cover over the spare wheel, and a rear bumper was an extra-cost option.

To complete the picture, there was the customary sliding roof, a tinted glass rear window, an opening windscreen, louvres over the side windows and an opening rear quarter-window to facilitate ventilation. The car had built-in direction indicators, a fog lamp, a stop lamp and a reversing light, as well as a rev-counter and the familiar Rover petrol gauge, which doubled as an oil level gauge. To flatter the driver, the manufacturers provided a tool kit in a tray housed under the bonnet.

Of course, there was more to the Wilks brothers' adoption of the Carbodies design than good business acumen. The Hastings Coupe appealed to them because it had that rare blend of elegance and style without a trace of flamboyance. This was precisely the image they wanted to achieve for Rovers, and elements of the Hastings Coupe design were to reappear in Rover's own bodies throughout the 1930s and right up until the demise of the P3 models in 1949. In the meantime, the underslung chassis frame was to be introduced as part of the Company's new model package for the 1934 season.

The first Wilks range: 10hp (1933-1938), 12hp, 14hp and Speed 14 (1933-1936)

The first complete range of Wilks-approved cars was introduced in the autumn of 1933. The cars were not, however, the only Rover models available for the 1934 season. Although production seems to have stopped in the summer of 1933, the Meteor 16 and Speed 20 models, derived from the earlier 2-litre/Light Six and Meteor/Light Twenty chassis, continued to be catalogued for 1934. The Meteor 16 was available only as a Saloon, while the Speed 20 could have Sports Tourer or Hastings Coupe coachwork.

A precise statement of the facts is dogged by the absence of factory records, but it seems that very few of these 'old stock' cars were sold during the 1934 season, the suggested total of 48 Meteor 16s giving an indication of the overall picture. By the autumn of 1934, the Meteors had all gone, but the Speed 20 was still on offer (although not catalogued), and the price reduction of £10 on a Hastings Coupe in the face of rising prices of other Rover models hints that Rover were anxious to dispose of the last of these

A 1934 12hp Tourer, photographed during 1981 at a Rover Sports Register meeting.

Rear view of the same car, showing the covered spare wheel. The flashing trafficators and the reflectors are both modern additions.

cars. Exactly how long they lingered is a matter for speculation, but it would be surprising if many remained unsold after the end of December 1934.

Chassis and engines

There were three basic varieties in the new Rover range for 1934 – the 10, 12 and 14. They were distinguished from their predecessors by underslung rear frames, by new engines in the case of the 10 and 12, and by the harmonic stabilizer incorporated in the front bumper. The 14 gained the longer-wheelbase, underslung-rear chassis of the previous season's Speed 14 model, so that only the Speed 14 was really carried over from 1933. All models came with four-speed constant-mesh gearboxes with 'silent' (helical-toothed) second and third gears, and all had a driver-controlled freewheel in the transmission.

The new engines in the 10 and 12 were the result of collaboration between Maurice Wilks and Robert Boyle. Spencer Wilks had called for a basic design which could be made to cover the whole range of sizes from 10hp to 20hp

by varying the bore diameter and the number of cylinders, with the obvious advantages of cost-saving in development and tooling. It was a plan which many other British car manufacturers followed in the 1930s. The new '100mm' engine – so named after the length of its stroke, which would remain a common feature of all variants – featured a three-bearing crankshaft and overhead valves at a time when the majority of medium-sized cars still had side-valve engines. Although the six-cylinder variant had already been sketched up, only 'fours' appeared in 1933. This was partly for reasons of financial prudence, and partly perhaps because the market for 16hp and larger cars had not yet stabilized after the Depression. The 14's six-cylinder engine, of course, was of relatively recent introduction and did not yet need to be replaced.

The new power units were advertised as 'high-efficiency OHV engines mounted in specially designed flexible mountings and giving an output of smooth, silent power, approximately four times their rating', although the latter claim was, in all fairness, a little optimistic! In 1,389cc form,

the '100mm' unit powered the 10hp model, replacing the previous season's ancient 1,185cc engine, which traced its origins back to the early 1920s. In larger-bore 1,496cc form it allowed the introduction of a model absent from the Rover range since 1932 – a 12hp.

The two four-cylinder chassis featured a new Girling rod-operated braking system, which seems a retrograde step after the Lockheed hydraulic system inherited by the 14 from the previous season's Speed 14 Pilot, but it received much praise from the motoring press. The press also enthused over the Wilmot-Breeden harmonic stabilizer, which had been introduced as a way of preventing the front end of the chassis frame from twisting – a problem to which it had been particularly prone ever since the flexible engine mountings introduced in 1932 had removed a large proportion of the frame's torsional stiffness. The harmonic stabilizer was actually a very long transverse leaf spring mounted behind the front bumper. Heavy bob-weights were attached to its extremities, and these in turn were concealed inside the end rolls of the bumper. In theory, the device

The Streamline models were typical of the 1930s' approach to aerodynamics. This Saloon demonstrates what the streamlining meant – just a curved rear panel.

damped out torsional movements of the front of the frame induced by rough road surfaces – and *The Autocar* staff proved to their own satisfaction that it worked by removing the stabilizer from their road-test 14 Saloon and observing the difference over a rough road. The harmonic stabilizer was copied by a number of other manufacturers in the 1930s, and indeed Rover remained faithful to the device until the introduction of a more rigid chassis frame for the P3 models rendered it unnecessary.

Rovers had first been fitted with the Lucas Startix system in 1932, and the unit was retained for the new model range. The Startix provided automatic restarting when the engine stalled if the clutch pedal was depressed. The automatic circuit was activated when the dynamo stopped charging – a feature which could have disastrous results if the dynamo failed while the car was in motion! Later varieties had a vacuum-operated safety switch attached to the inlet manifold, but even that did not eradicate the system's bad name, and Rover ceased to fit it in 1936.

The principal change for 1935 was the introduction on all

models of a Luvax-Bijur centralized chassis lubrication system, which was intended to reduce maintenance. An oil reservoir mounted on the bulkhead was connected to a series of small-diameter pipes, which ducted oil to 23 chassis lubrication points at a single touch on a hand-operated plunger, pressure being supplied by inlet manifold vacuum. In practice, the pipes tended to become clogged unless as much maintenance was given to the automatic lubrication system as would otherwise have been given to the chassis! Nevertheless, Rover persisted with the system until the end of 1947. The 1935 10s, 12s and 14s all had 'automatic voltage control' – which meant voltage-controlled battery charging – and a new Burman Douglas steering box in place of the earlier Marles Weller unit, while the 1,577cc engine of the 14hp models benefited from a raised compression ratio and from streamlined ports and manifolds. This change was largely precipitated by the exceptional performance of the 12, which was very nearly a match for the 14 in 1934 guise; model differentials had to be maintained at all costs! For 1935, the 12 came in two wheelbase lengths, the longer of which was new to the model and used the Speed 14's chassis frame. That model remained unchanged with its 112in wheelbase, but the basic 14 gained a new chassis with a 115in wheelbase, which helped to distinguish it further from the 12. The 1935 Speed 14 was announced and catalogued with coil-spring independent front suspension (apparently developed from Porsche's 1931 torsion-bar system, which later went into production in the VW Beetle). Although prototypes with IFS were seen at the Company's Seagrave Road Service Depot in London, production cars all had the familiar semi-elliptic springing for reasons which remain obscure. (At a guess, the chassis frame was too flexible at the front to allow the IFS system to work properly). Gordon Bashford remembers further experiments with an alternative IFS layout known as the 'Nutcracker', but independent front suspension would not appear on a production Rover until 1948.

Changes for 1936 were limited to the adoption of Lucas special electrical equipment on all four models, and the fitting of Girling rod-operated brakes to the 14s to bring them into line with the smaller-engined chassis. The 14, however, could now be ordered with the Speed 14's triple-carburettor engine, high-compression head, sports exhaust system and 4·8:1 axle, while the 12 could have a twin-carburettor engine with high-compression head and a sports exhaust, which gave it a performance equal to that of the standard 14. In practice, it seems that these options remained rare.

Bodies

The separate-chassis construction of 1930s cars meant that manufacturers could fit a variety of different bodies to the same chassis. It was also common practice to offer not only complete cars for sale, but also the chassis only for fitment with specialist bodywork by an outside coachbuilder. Obviously, this was not common on the cheaper models by manufacturers like Ford, Austin or Morris, but Rover customers could buy all the company's models in chassis-only form, the 10hp included. There were, of course, certain 'approved' bodies, and the Hastings Coupe was one of these.

The factory-produced bodies offered an impressive varie-ty. Six-light Saloon bodies, a four-light Sports Saloon and a four-light fixed-head Coupe were offered on the 10, 12 and 14 chassis for 1934, while an open Tourer was available on all these plus the Speed 14 chassis. In addition, the Speed 14 could be fitted with the four-light Hastings Coupe body. For the 1935 and 1936 seasons, however, this variety was cut back quite dramatically, so that fewer bodies were offered on the smaller-engined chassis; although five different body types were still available, the 10 came only as a six-light Saloon, and the 12s only as a six-light Saloon on the long-wheelbase chassis or a four-light Sports Saloon on the short chassis. The six-light Saloon body was also available on the 14, as was the four-light Sports Saloon. The Coupes and Hastings Coupe disappeared altogether, and the Tourer was restricted to the Speed 14 chassis. New 'Streamline' bodies – a six-light Saloon and a four-light Coupe – were available on the 14 and Speed 14 chassis.

It is interesting to see how much these bodies were a reflection of the Wilks philosophy which had first become evident in the 1932-season cars. Rovers were to appeal to the British professional man (there was no export market to consider), whose needs and aspirations Spencer Wilks understood only too well. Richard Hough and Michael Frostick summed it up very well in their book *Rover Memories:* 'If the typical Rover owner was not from the upper strata of the middle classes (and many of them were), he was made to feel that he was.'

Thus the emphasis was on interior comfort and the quality of appointments; there were well-sprung leather seats set off by polished wood for the dashboard and door cappings. The bodies were roomy, with wide-opening doors, and their outward appearance was discreet – even in the case of the short-lived Streamline bodies – and conservative, bearing witness to superior taste and without a trace of flamboyance. They were well-equipped, too, the 1935 10 Saloon, for example, having an interior light, a driving mirror, ashtrays, side armrests, rope pulls, pile carpets, a rear window blind, a sliding roof and a roof parcel net as standard. All cars except the 10 came with a fitted tool kit, which was located under the bonnet of Tourers and Sports Saloons, but in a tray under the dashboard of six-light Saloon bodies.

The Streamline Coupes were much prettier, but scarcely more successful in sales terms. The centre-lock wire wheels were standard equipment on all Speed 14s, and optional on other models during 1936.

Although standardization was well under way, the Rover-built bodies of 1933-36 encompassed an astonishing complexity of variants. The six-light Saloon bodies appear very similar, but there were actually three varieties, one shared by the 12 and the 14, and the other two unique to the 10. The 10 Saloon's body, of course, traced its ancestry back to the Hillman Minx-derived pressed-steel body of 1931, while the body of the 12 and 14 was basically that of the 1933 Pilot with a more curved rear roofline, front doors hinged on the centre pillars and a more flowing rear wing line than the 10. These bodies added sun visors, an opening rear quarter-window and a folding central armrest on the rear seat to the specification of the 10 quoted previously. Although the 14 was distinguished from the 12 by its slightly longer wheelbase, the extra 3in were absorbed in the bonnet area with the result that the bodies were of identical dimensions. From the autumn of 1934, all Saloon bodies incorporated a new steel bulkhead and, the following year, all gained louvres over the drop-glasses to match those already fitted to the Sports Saloons.

The 10 Saloon's body lasted two years longer than those of the 12 and 14 models, but for the 1937 season its rear roofline was altered to resemble the earlier 12 and 14, and the front doors were hinged on the centre pillar. All the Saloon bodies had the spare wheel mounted on their flat rear panel, the 10s having a plain metal disc cover until the close

of the 1936 season, and then inheriting from the 12 and 14 a neat contoured fairing over the wheel. There was no luggage boot, but a trunk could be strapped to the drop-down luggage grid at the rear when touring.

The Sports Saloons were unashamedly four-door derivatives of Carbodies' Hastings Coupe design. Lower than the six-light Saloons, they were also shorter, so that from 1935 the 12 Sports Saloon used the short-wheelbase chassis, identical in dimensions to that of the 10; the 14's extra wheelbase, of course, was occupied by its engine. Although the Sports Saloons gave away almost nothing in headroom, legroom in the rear was considerably less than in the Saloons. As witness that they were designed for touring, the Sports Saloon bodies had an enclosed boot behind the rear seats. The spare wheel was mounted beneath a metal cover on the drop-down lid of this boot, which could be used as a platform if oversize loads were to be carried. Only 50 Sports Saloons were built on the 10 chassis, and all were sold through Henly's, in London. As for the two-door Coupe, which was actually a carryover from the 1933 season, it was fundamentally similar to the Hastings Coupe, differing visually in the absence of louvres over the drop-glasses and in certain other minor respects. It was available during the 1934 season only, on the 10, 12 and 14 chassis, and remained rare.

The Tourers (Open Tourers for the more mundane

Rover offered chassis for the fitting of custom-built bodies until the close of the 1937 season. This is a Tickford drophead saloon body, built by Salmons & Sons, of Newport Pagnell, and shown here on a 1934 14hp chassis.

chassis, but a Sports Tourer on the Speed 14 chassis) were two-door, four-seater bodies with a collapsible hood and detachable sidescreens. Their ancestry lay in the tourer bodies built by outside concerns for the pre-1934 chassis, such as the Rajah Semi-sports four-seater, but their design was pleasantly rakish where those bodies had been rather uninspired. A nice touch was the cutaway top to the doors, so that young bloods could comfortably drive with one elbow nonchalantly resting on the door frame! These models brought to open-air motoring in the 1930s a refinement which was not be to be found in the more overtly sporting tourers with which they competed, principally because they used chassis which had been designed for more sedate purposes. Perhaps it was this as much as anything which ensured that they were not a great commercial success. They were too refined for the wind-in-the-hair sporting motorist of the 1930s, and for 1936 their availability was reduced to the 12 chassis only. Probably no more than 150 were built between 1933 and 1936, although their cult appeal was eventually such that they were the sole reason for the foundation in 1953 of the oldest of the Rover enthusiasts' clubs, the Rover Sports Register.

The Streamline bodies were the result of a curious mid-1930s fashion which produced such notable designs as the *Coronation Scot* and A4 Pacific streamlined express

railway locomotives as well as a host of grotesque machines which are best forgotten. In the motoring world, the pioneer was Chrysler's Airflow saloon, and the fashion, but not the research, was imitated in the UK by Triumph and SS, among others. Like these other manufacturers, Rover designed bodies which paid lip-service to streamlining, but were aerodynamically no better than the more conventional closed bodies, and may indeed have been worse! The airflow characteristics of the Rover bodies were certainly very strange; during development, it was found that exhaust fumes were sucked into ventilation louvres let into the back panel and into the front quarter-lights! Production models dispensed with the louvres and featured drop-glasses at the front in place of the swivelling quarter-lights.

All the streamlining, and indeed all the interest, of these bodies was at the rear. With the benefit of hindsight and modern terminology, they can be more accurately described as 'fastback' styles. Seating was not affected by the sloping rear panels, although there was a recess in the headlining over the rear seat to ensure adequate headroom. The space created behind the top of the rear seat became a parcel shelf, which was fortunate because the headroom precluded use of a roof parcel net. Below that, the body widened out to furnish an enclosed boot with a drop-down lid; and at the apex of the rear panel, the spare wheel lay flat beneath the boot in its own special compartment, reached from outside the car.

There were two Streamline body types, of which the Coupe was by far the more elegant, its four-light design blending nicely with the streamlined tail; the Saloon, by contrast, looked awkward with its rearmost side window sitting uncomfortably behind the doors. Its rear panel swept down less gracefully, with the result that the 'fastback' was grafted incongruously onto a rather upright-looking body. Not surprisingly, the Coupe was the more popular of the two styles.

Body shapes apart, there were small details which allowed one Rover model to be distinguished from the next. Thus the 1934 cars all had black-painted wings regardless of the body colour, while the bonnet sides incorporated vertical louvres. On the 10s and 14s there were five groups of six louvres, while the 12s had only four groups. The black wings disappeared for 1935, and two-tone colour finishes became available. The vertical bonnet louvres were replaced on 1936 models by horizontal louvres, and for 1937 and 1938 the 10s had deeper front wings which extended lower and met the bonnet sides higher up. Streamline bodies were only ever available in single colours.

All models had wire wheels, although it was possible to fit wheel discs to give the appearance of solid wheels. Knock-on wire wheels by Rudge-Whitworth were available as an option for 1936, and were standard on the Speed 14 throughout. The 1935-36 Speed 14 also had its headlamps and pass lamp mounted on a tripod ahead of the radiator, while all other models had headlamps alongside the radiator. The horn was mounted under the bonnet of the 10s, but on the offside dumb-iron of 12s and 14s, when it was matched by a pass lamp on the nearside dumb-iron. Chromed twin horns were fitted between the radiator grille and the bumper of Speed 14s, and were optionally available on other models. 1936 season Tourers and Sports Saloons were recognizable by a fuel filler cap moved from the boot to the wing. All the

Streamline bodies came with a Brooklands-type fishtail exhaust, while Sports Saloons and Coupes had no rear bumper unless to special order. As contemporary sales literature shows, however, Rover were prepared to fit practically anything to special order, at a price!

The lack of records makes it difficult to establish now how many of these first Wilks models were fitted with coachwork by outside concerns, or even what bodies were available. Few examples survive today, and such cars are certainly rare, if not always desirable beasts. Two examples of coachbuilt bodies may be cited: Salmons of Newport Pagnell offered their Tickford body (a sort of drophead Saloon) on the 12, 14 and Speed 14 chassis, while Midland Light Motor Bodies offered the rather angular Melba, an open tourer for the man who wanted four doors rather than the two of the standard Rover Tourer.

By the time the revised range appeared in 1936, Rover were once again on a firm footing. Since 1933, the Company had expanded steadily, and a net profit of £156,282 was recorded for the season 1935-36, with Rover taking 2.35 per cent of the British market and building 8,335 cars. In April 1936, Rover were one of the few car manufacturers selected by the Government to participate in the 'shadow factory' scheme, and this evidence of their new standing was echoed in the ease with which they were able to raise an extra £260,000 capital in 1937. Almost all of this change had been brought about by the success of the Wilks' first model range, a total of 21,231 cars having been built since their introduction in 1933. Sales demand was strong: *Light Car* magazine reported on August 21, 1936: 'It is scarcely a secret that the entire 1936 output was sold some time ago'. The Rover image was now well established as that of a manufacturer of well-built, well-engineered, well-equipped and reliable medium-sized cars, which were generally able to show a clean pair of heels to their rivals of similar price and capacity, in spite of their conservative appearance. For Rover in 1936, the sky must have seemed the limit.

CHAPTER 2

One of Britain's Fine Cars

Elegance and refinement, 1936 – 1947

Revised 10hp (1938-1940), 12hp and 14hp (1937-1940); 16hp (1936-1940), Speed Model (1936-1937) and 20hp (1937-1940); 10hp, 12hp 14hp and 16hp (1945-1947)

Spencer Wilks was able to put phase two of his six-year plan into operation in the autumn of 1936. This involved the substitution for the rather variegated range of bodies of two basic body styles which would fit all the available chassis. In simple terms, the savings gained from the standardization of body types permitted the introduction of two new six-cylinder chassis. The net result was to be a range of cars which covered a wider market, from the 10hp to the 20hp, and one which also had a clear family identity. Rover marketed them under the slogan 'One of Britain's Fine Cars'.

Chassis and engines

Of the chassis beneath the new bodies introduced for the 1937 season, only two were actually carried over from the four available for 1936. These were the 12hp and the 14hp. The capital available for tooling still had to be carefully apportioned, and so the 10hp car was not updated to the new specification, but remained in its earlier form for another two seasons. Meanwhile, the Speed 14 disappeared entirely, to be replaced at the top of the Rover range by the two new six-cylinder chassis, the 16hp and Speed Model (later 20hp).

Development of the new six-cylinder chassis actually started before the earlier 16s and 20s went out of production in 1933. The '100mm' engine introduced in the 1934 cars had been designed as a 'stretchable' unit, and a six-cylinder variant was certainly on the drawing-board, if not actually running, by the middle of 1933. However, Maurice Wilks wanted to keep his options open, and in 1934-35 he asked his engine designers to look into the feasibility of vee-configurations, with the idea that such an engine might go into the forthcoming 16 and 20hp models. Jack Swaine, who was then a young engineer but would later head Rover's engine design team, recalls that Wilks wanted an engine which was no longer than the four-cylinder '100mm' unit. Clearly, if the additional length of the '100mm six' could be avoided, it would be possible to use exactly the same chassis for both four and six-cylinder cars.

Whatever the reasons for Wilks' request, Rover's engine designers sketched up a 60-degree V8 unit as a first attempt. That design never progressed beyond paper, and the next proposal was for a 90-degree V6. Jack Swaine recalls the designers' pride on their invention of a new configuration, and their subsequent disappointment on learning that diesel engines with this layout had been in existence for some time! The V6 design, which was largely Swaine's work, was dictated very much by the narrow bonnets of the cars then in production; whatever chassis alterations may have been under consideration, the bonnet size looked as if it would stay the same. Swaine decided to use a single camshaft in the centre of the vee, operating directly on to side exhaust valves and via pushrods to overhead inlet valves. The vee design took care of length considerations, but to keep the width down Swaine decided to tip the angle of the top face

This shot of Rover's entries for the 1937 RAC Rally makes an interesting comparison between the old and the new models. Differences are most apparent in the shape of the front wings. The Tourer of course, is a Speed model with the special head-lamp and horn arrangement and the centre-lock wire wheels. The 1937 model alongside is a six-light Saloon.

of the cylinder block towards the centre of the engine.

In the event, the V6 never went beyond the prototype stage, and the 16hp and 20hp chassis introduced in the autumn of 1936 were powered by a six-cylinder derivative of the '100mm four', exactly as planned earlier. Swaine's work was not wasted, however. Maurice Wilks was impressed by the combustion chamber design of the V6, and asked him to incorporate the sloping-head, inlet-over-exhaust configuration into an in-line engine. The resulting four-cylinder prototype was the first in a series which would lead, many years later, to the all-new IOE engines of the P3 cars.

So the 1937 season 16 used a 2,147cc six-cylinder version of the '100mm' engine, while the Speed Model used an even larger 2,512cc variant. They had the same new chassis, which shared its basic design and many components with that of the smaller-engined cars, but had been considerably strengthened at the front to cope with the additional strains imposed by the big six-cylinder engines. Both had the steering box mounted ahead of the axle and both shared the 115in wheelbase of the 14, but with the track an inch wider at 52in. Their DWS hydraulic jacking system, with the jacks built into the chassis frame, would be extended in 1938 to the 14 as well. The 14 and the 12 remained mechanically identical to the previous season's models, with the exception that the 12's wheels were down-sized to 17in, leaving only the 10 with 18in wheels. All models, the unrevised 10 included, had new hubcaps – 'nave-plates' as Rover liked to call them - with the Company name emblazoned across the middle. There were no significant changes for the 1938 season, except that Easy Clean pressed-steel disc wheels became available as an option in place of the standard wires, and the Speed Model was renamed a 20hp, which made better sense as it was aimed at the prestige market rather than the sporting motorist. The disc wheels had a new hubcap with a small disc in the centre bearing an enamelled Rover emblem. A 10hp Coupe with a body of the same family as the new styles became available alongside the old 10hp Saloon, but it boasted no chassis differences apart from its 17in wheels.

Perhaps the biggest change for 1939 was the replacement of the 14's 1,577cc Pilot engine by a new six-cylinder untit of 1,901cc which belonged to the '100mm' family. Despite the increase in swept volume, the new engine was rated by the RAC at only 14.9hp, so there was some justification for the retention of the '14' designation, even if the car was now more expensive to licence (it counted as a 15hp). Despite a weight increase of some 300lb over the 1938 14hp, the new model had generally comparable acceleration, plus a higher top speed.

The 1939 season also saw a number of chassis changes. The 10hp Saloon gained an extra half-inch in its wheelbase and 17in wheels to go with its new-style body, with the

All finishing work was carried out by hand. Here, six-light bodyshells are being rubbed down prior to the application of the first colour coat. These are postwar models, photographed at Solihull in 1946.

result that none of the earlier range now remained in production. An extra 2in was inserted into the rear track of 16hp models to give a wider rear seat, and new Luvax piston-type shock absorbers were standardized right across the range together with Easy Clean wheels, although wires remained available at extra cost. Steering and control on the six-cylinder cars were improved by the use of anti-roll torsion bars at the front and rear. On the engine side, the four-cylinder models, 10hp and 12hp, gained a new eight-port cylinder head in place of the earlier six-port component and this, in combination with a raised compression ratio, increased power. There was a redesigned cooling system for all five models, and provision was made for the first time for a passenger-compartment heater which, however, was an extra-cost option. No doubt the public were impressed by the addition of synchromesh to third and fourth gears of all gearboxes for 1939, although it must be said that the freewheel still fitted as standard made this bow in the direction of Rover's rivals altogether unnecessary.

Changes in specification had already entered production before the outbreak of war in September 1939, but there were relatively few 1940-season cars. Production limped along while the Rover factories were gradually changed over to the production of aircraft parts, and the last 'prewar' car came off the production lines in May 1940. The six-cylinder engines for 1940 had redesigned porting and higher compression ratios to parallel the changes introduced on the 1939 four-cylinder engines, and this provided an extra 10 per cent power with a 20 per cent increase in low-speed torque. To cope with these extra loads, shell bearings were fitted to both mains and big-ends. A twin-choke down-draught Solex carburettor was also standardized on the six-cylinder cars in place of the earlier SU. The chassis of the 10 remained unchanged for 1940, but the 12 gained the anti-roll bars of the six-cylinder models, and its rear track was widened in common with the previous season's 16hp.

The Helen Street factory was bombed into ruins by the Luftwaffe on November 14, 1940, and so when the war ended and private car production was again sanctioned by the Government, the Rover Company moved lock, stock and

A 1938 14hp six-light Saloon, seen in 1981. Bonnet sides are plain, unlike those of the 1937 model illustrated on page 22.

The 'box boot' was characteristic of both the four-light and six-light bodies.

barrel into the much larger 'shadow' factory at Solihull which they had occupied during the hostilities. Helen Street was patched up and sold, and the Company's designers settled down to the awesome task of catching up on three years' worth of advances in automotive engineering from across the Atlantic. In the meantime, it was vital to get production started again and to have cars in the showrooms. There were obviously no new models ready, and so Spencer Wilks ordered that the prewar models should go back into production. He and Maurice Wilks allocated them the code number P1 – for the first postwar car – although this was not a designation which was commonly used outside Rover's engineering departments.

Things could not be quite the same again, however. Materials shortages were the order of the day, and the economic climate favoured small cars rather than large ones. Indeed, Rover's first steel allocation permit specified 500 10hp, 500 12hp and only 100 six-cylinder cars, together with eight development or prototype vehicles. Against such a background, it was inevitable that the six-cylinder range

By 1947, when this 16hp Sports Saloon was built, Easyclean disc wheels were standard. The photographer was Alan Milstead.

should be cut back, and so the reintroduced range was shorn of the most expensive 20hp model and only the 10, 12, 14 and 16hp chassis went back into production. Government policy was also geared towards exports and the 'export or die' requirement came hard to a company like Rover, whose sole concession to overseas markets had been the fitting of larger wheels and tyres to 'Colonial' models in the 1930s. Tom Barton was later to make his mark on the Land-Rover, but his first job after the war was to design the modifications necessary for the very first left-hand-drive Rovers.

Feverish design activity at Solihull managed to get these modifications and a redesigned gearbox for all models into production within a matter of months, although at first only the 16hp Saloon was available with left-hand-drive, the Sports Saloon and 10hp Saloon following for the 1947 season. The official opening of the Solihull factory took place on February 2, 1946, when the ceremony was performed by Sir Stafford Cripps, then President of the Board of Trade, but the press had already carried photographs of the first postwar Rovers – two 10hp models

– leaving the factory in December 1945. Generally speaking the specification of the P1 models followed that of the 1940 cars, although prices had spiralled upwards and were further inflated by a hefty Purchase Tax. Rampant inflation also had its effect in the early postwar years, and the basic price (without Purchase Tax) of a 10hp Saloon went up by 30 percent in the 15 months between December 1945 and March 1947. Not surprisingly, very few changes were made during the two seasons of P1 production, as Solihull's efforts were directed towards designing entirely new models in preference to facelifting the old. In the event, P1 production actually lasted some six months longer than planned when the Land-Rover held up introduction of the replacement models in 1947. The last P1s left the production lines before Christmas 1947, after which retooling began for the production of the P3 models for introduction in February 1948.

Bodies
Although the 1937-season models were offered for sale in

25

Dashboard of a 1947 model. The large turnwheel control operated the freewheel, and the winder in the centre of the facia rail opened the windscreen. The two knobs below this worked the windscreen wipers; the passenger-side arm could be switched out when not required. Note also the under-dash tool tray, just visible on the left, and the footwell air vent. The badge at the base of the instrument panel reads 'Coachwork by Rover'; P3 and later bodies were built by Pressed Steel.

chassis-only form, and it was possible to obtain chassis to special order in later years, very few of the 1939-47 cars were ever fitted with non-standard coachwork. The early 1930s had been the dying years of the smaller coachbuilding concerns in Britain, as the effects of the Depression spread through the motor industry. By the mid-1930s, the professional man no longer bought a coachbuilt body for his chosen chassis as a matter of course; he settled for the body offered by the chassis manufacturer. With the revised Rover range for 1937, even the splendid variety of the early Wilks cars' Rover-built bodies disappeared, although it must be said that the two new bodies introduced in the autumn of 1936 were of extremely high quality and pleasing to the eye, so that the loss was not readily apparent. As sales figures show, there was certainly no reluctance among Rover's customers to accept this restriction on their choice of body styles.

To many eyes, the late 1930s Rover Saloon and Sports Saloon bodies represent the pinnacle of that decade's saloon car elegance. Far more modern in appearance than the rather upright closed bodies of their predecessors, they were nevertheless conventional in conception, and this happy mixture of old and new gave them an air of timelessness. What is perhaps most astonishing about them is that they were designed by mechanical engineers and not by stylists at all.

Ever since the appearance of Carbodies' Hastings Coupe in 1932, Spencer and Maurice Wilks had known which way they wanted Rover body styling to go. As chief of design and engineering, it fell to Maurice to execute the styling, but this was something which he felt to be beyond his skills as a mechanical engineer. So he took on Harry Loker as a kind of amanuensis. He knew that he wanted the new designs to bear the imprint of the Hastings Coupe; achieving that aim

26

A 1948 12hp Tourer, with hood and sidescreens erected. Compare this with the earlier pictures of the 1934 Tourer.

was Loker's business. The new bodies were drafted out between the two men, with Loker turning Maurice Wilks' ideas and wishes into reality.

The line of development from Hastings Coupe through the 1933-36 Sports Saloons and on to the 1937-season Rover bodies is clearly visible. The 1937-season Sports Saloon was really a softer-contoured version of its immediate predecessor, aided by the impression of length given by its sleeker wings. Perhaps the most noticeable common feature dating back to the Hastings design was the square and practical 'box boot', tidier on the 1937-season bodies with the spare wheel recessed into the drop-down lid and easily accessible from inside when required, yet shielded from the actual luggage compartment by a simple cover. The circular impression on the boot lid which betrays the spare wheel's position on the 1937 bodies also provided an attractive styling element at the rear of the body. The 1937 six-light Saloon, more upright and slightly taller than the Sports Saloon, turned the same basic design into an elegant but not quite formal body, offering more spacious accommodation,

yet with the family resemblance to the Sports Saloon clearly visible in every panel. Both bodies had a gently raked windscreen, with pleasantly curved edges giving a less stark appearance than that of earlier cars.

Rover themselves actually made more of the new wing-line which went with these bodies than of what they simply called the 'New Silent Coachwork', expressing the difference thus: 'The front wings are larger and stronger and are mounted high up the side of the radiator. A wide inside valance is provided and the wing is lower at its front edge. A deeper outside valance combined with a wider section gives greater effective coverage to the wheel. The rear wings are also deeper and wider in section, and terminate with an extended valance.' The 'helmet' shape of the front wings is in fact an easy recognition point of these post-1936 cars.

The doors of these steel-panelled bodies built on ash frames opened wide to make access easy, and this feature no doubt attracted many of the elderly customers who seemed to make up more and more of Rover's clientele in the later 1930s. The Company made much in its advertising of the

A 1938 10hp Coupe, fitted with the optional covers over its wire wheels. Later models had plain bonnet sides.

From behind, the 10hp Coupe was instantly recognizable because it lacked the spare wheel impression on its boot lid.

fact that the rear seats were within the wheelbase, thus leading to greater riding comfort, while the long wheelbases ensured that even in the less generously proportioned Sports Saloons there was still plenty of legroom for rear seat passengers. Upholstery, of course, was in soft leather, and there were substantial armrests in the rear compartment, of a less ornamental design than in earlier bodies. A rear window blind could be pulled up by a cord reaching to the driver's position, and Saloon bodies had a parcels net in the roof to keep bulky items from under the passengers' feet. Sliding roofs were still *de rigueur* in this class, and both Saloons and Sports Saloons had them. The tool kit was now fitted under the dash in all bodies. Both types of body were available on 12, 14 and 16hp chassis, while only the Saloon was offered on the 10hp chassis (from autumn 1938) and only the Sports Saloon could be had on the 20hp chassis.

The two basic bodies were joined by a third in the autumn of 1937 when the 10hp received its first new-style body. The newcomer was an extremely pretty little two-door Coupe, again styled by Maurice Wilks and Harry Loker,

The spare wheel impression at the rear of the drophead bodies differed from that of the Rover-built bodies. Illustrated is a 1939 model 16hp or 20hp.

and echoing the Saloons and Sports Saloons in every way except that there was no spare wheel impression on its boot lid. Although it never sold in large quantities, the 10 Coupe remains one of the most attractive of the late 1930s Rovers. The body range was further broadened for the 1939 season when a drophead coupe style was made available for the six-cylinder chassis. This two-door body was designed and built by Salmons of Newport Pagnell, but retained a Rover family trademark in the spare wheel impression on its boot lid. Its high price probably contributed to the low sales volume, but the Salmons-bodied Rovers remain desirable cars today, 1940 models being distinguishable from 1939 cars by the addition of quarter-lights to the front of the doors.

The 1938 season saw improved side and centre armrests in the closed bodies, while the rear compartment ashtrays were repositioned in the front seat backs. Steel-reinforced rear quarters made it possible to provide additional headroom, and the seats of all except the 10hp bodies were improved two years later by the introduction of a new air-cell rubber cushioning material. As the wider rear track arrived, so the rear seats were widened into the space provided. Autumn 1939 also witnessed the arrival of larger dashboard instruments, and the petrol reserve control became a dashboard switch instead of a tap under the boot floor. There was a new spring-spoke steering wheel, and wood capping was added to the windscreen rail to give a rather more opulent appearance, while the 10 gained louvres over its side windows to match the six-light bodies on larger-engined chassis. Postwar bodies were identical to the 1940 models, although the cutbacks which had to be made meant that the 10's Coupe body and the dropheads were no longer available. The final year's production from January 1947 had Clayton-Dewandre heater/demister units as standard, facia changes to permit the installation of the optional radio under the centre and a thermostatically-controlled choke warning light in place of the trafficator telltale.

As usual, Rover provided a comprehensive range of extra-cost options. In the autumn of 1937, for example, it was possible to specify two different types of spring-spoke

The Viking's head mascot was a feature of 1929 season Rovers. The Company produced a second edition of 2,000 in 1946, priced at two guineas each, and the Rover Sports Register has arranged for further reproductions to be made. Although often fitted by enthusiasts, they are not an authentic feature of the 1930s cars. Photograph by Alan Milstead.

steering wheel, a badge bar, two fitted suitcases in the boot and twin horns with a crossbar-mounted pass lamp on all models except the 20, which had the suitcases and twin horn arrangement as standard anyway. On the 10 and 12, the oil gauge could be replaced by a combined water temperature and oil pressure gauge, and all models could have adjustable armrests on the front doors, a cigarette lighter, an inspection lamp plug, a master battery switch, a compact Philips radio with an under-chassis aerial, and even knock-on wire wheels if the customer insisted. Two-tone paint was phased out as a standard option with the 1937 models, but it continued to be available at extra cost for 1938. Postwar cars were all single-tone, and at first were available only in black with brown upholstery.

It is pleasing to record that the postwar restrictions and conditions actually led to the appearance of a new body style. This was a Tourer, available on the 12 chassis during 1947 and theoretically for export only. However, as all the Tourer bodies were fitted to right-hand-drive chassis, a number not surprisingly found their way on to the home market! A rumour persists that some Tourer bodies were fitted to 10hp chassis, although neither records nor actual cars have ever been found to substantiate this.

The Tourer bodies shared almost none of the lines of the contemporary closed bodies, and the story which is told of their conception explains why. Once the decision had been made to build a Tourer, Maurice Wilks had to design it, and with his characteristic diffidence about designing a new body from scratch, he decided that the new Tourer would have to be based on the 1934-36 Tourers. Unfortunately, Rover's body drawings had been destroyed during the war, and so he set about finding a prewar Tourer to use as a pattern. The Rover Company duly bought back a 1934 12hp Tourer, registered JN4364, which is thought to have aquired the later 17in wire wheels while in their ownership (the postwar Tourers, of course, would have the contemporary 17in disc wheels). This car, incidentally, was owned by a member of the Rover Sports Register for many years until its purchase by a New Zealand enthusiast, who exported it to his home country, where it is believed still to be.

Although Maurice Wilks based the new Tourer body on the 1934-36 design, he did not copy it slavishly. For a start, the smaller wheels and deeper wings of the postwar cars made a difference to the proportions, and Wilks and Harry Loker decided on a new rear-end treatment, without the enclosed spare wheel. Regrettably, the rather upright wings and bonnet of the postwar model and its standard disc wheels seemed to take away much of the sporting character of the design, which was otherwise notable for its use of a metal cover over the hood well. Not many of these rather pretty cars were made before production ceased at the end of 1947.

Certain recognition features help to distinguish one model of the 1936-47 range from another. The 1937 models all had horizontal louvres in the bonnet sides, as did the 1938 10

Coupes, but from 1938 the 12s, 14s, 16s and 20s, and from 1939 both varieties of 10, had a new bonnet arrangement with detachable side panels and centre-hinged top panels. The 12s and 14s, and 10s from 1939, had plain side panels, while the 16s and 20s had two hinged flaps in each side. (Just to confuse the issue, however, 250 16hp Saloons and 50 16hp Sports Saloons built in 1947 had plain bonnet sides, probably in order to use up stocks of 14hp parts!) A fog or pass lamp was fitted to the nearside dumb-iron of all models except the 20s, which bore the lamp on a chromed triangular bracket ahead of the grille. The pass lamp was matched on the offside dumb-iron by a horn except on 20s, which had a horn on both dumb-irons. The 1940 Sports Saloons, Dropheads and 10 Coupes, and the postwar Tourers and

Sports Saloons shared the lamp and horn arrangement of the 20s. The 1939 and later models had an automatic reversing light combined with the nearside tail lamp and a single stop/tail lamp instead of the earlier twin stop/tail lamps, while there were also new torpedo-shaped side lamps with domed glasses, and a non-dipping headlamp system. With this system, 'dipping' the lights meant extinguishing the offside lamp and substituting the lower-aimed beam of the pass lamp, so called because its use permitted oncoming drivers to pass without being dazzled.

As noted earlier, there were very few custom-built bodies on the 1936-47 chassis, the excellence of the in-house product rendering them almost superfluous. At least one Martin Walter Wingham Cabriolet (more familar perhaps on

Vauxhall, Hillman or Daimler/Lanchester chassis) was fitted to a 16hp chassis during 1939, and allegedly there were three others like it. Perhaps there were other custom-built bodies, but Rover historians have so far failed to unearth any trace of them.

'Specials'

The Second World War took its toll of many of the early Wilks Rovers, and the years of enforced neglect meant that owners were often willing to part with their cars cheaply when peace came. Bodies generally deteriorated more than the mechanical components, and not surprisingly a few cars were rebodied while others were turned into 'trials specials' for the popular motor sport of the time.

Eleven 10hp and 12hp chassis (both pre- and post-1936) were given hand-built Tourer-type bodies during the 1950s and 1960s by one Rowley Kitcher of Newport, in what was then Monmouthshire. These Kitcher Specials had a two-seater aluminium body with cycle wings and a spare wheel mounted externally at the rear, and were provided with full weather protection from a hood and sidescreens. The lightweight body ensured that these vehicles had a sporting performance, and a Kitcher Special is now a highly desirable car in the eyes of many prewar Rover enthusiasts.

CHAPTER 3

Inlets over exhausts

The P3 gap-filler, 1948 – 1949

P3 60 and 75 (1948-1949)

Once the war was over and the Rover Company could legitimately think again in terms of new models, they were confronted by an awkward problem which faced all European manufacturers. American car design had not been interrupted by the hostilities until 1942, and was now three years ahead. The 1946-season American cars were radically different in appearance from the immediate prewar European models, and although they were few and far between on this side of the Atlantic, it was clear that all the advances of those three lost years had to be assimilated in record time if the new European models were not to look, and be, horribly dated in comparison.

Maurice Wilks' first serious plan was for a much modified P1, re-engined with a new IOE unit derived from Jack Swaine's V6 of the mid-1930s. This engine had been running in prototype four-cylinder form before the war, and could soon be brought up to production standard, although it was broader than the '100mm' OHV units, and so the P1 chassis frame would have to be widened at the front. As for the body, it would simply be the standard P1 style, widened and updated with a new front end based on the American styling trends of 1942. This meant a full-width front with wings blending into the radiator grille panel. Aided as usual by Harry Loker, Wilks tried out various styling modifications in clay on a full-size P1, but somehow a full-width front in the 1942 American idiom always looked comical grafted on to a prewar Rover passenger cabin. As Rover could not wait too long before putting a new model into the showrooms, Wilks abandoned the P2 project and decided to try something else.

There was no doubt in his mind that the new car should have an IOE engine with the existing production gearbox (which had recently been redesigned for the P1 models), but instead of rejigging the old underslung chassis frame Rover could use the new, more rigid frame which had been under development in 1939 and had run throughout the war in prototype form with the body of a 10hp. To this could be added independent front suspension, for work on such systems had continued after the installation planned for the 1935 Speed 14 had been abandoned. As there was no time to start work on a completely new body, the widened P1 body would have to do, with a nose design generally similar to the prewar one. This second attempt at a postwar Rover was different enough from the P2 concept to merit the new designation of P3.

As things were to turn out, designing the P3 was rather more complicated than it appeared at first sight, especially when Wilks decided to go for an all-steel body instead of the ash-framed type of P1s. Yet despite the major engineering changes which went into the P3, it was obvious to Rover from the outset that a car which looked so much like the prewar models could only be a stop-gap, even in the seller's market presented by a car-starved world in the early postwar years. Indeed, P3 production was to last no longer than 18 months.

Chassis and engines

'In order to gear production to the National need for

economy,' read the P3 sales catalogue, 'the Rover Company decided to produce one chassis model only with a choice of four- or six-cylinder engines.' That single chassis had a wheelbase of 110½in, midway between the wheelbase lengths of the P1 10 and 12 and considerably shorter than that of the superseded 14 and 16. Its track was an inch wider at the rear than that of the P1, while the front track was half-an-inch narrower. Although of massively rigid box-section construction, which obviated the need for the harmonic stabilizer, it was actually lighter than the P1 chassis because it reached only three-quarters of the way under the car; the side members stopped short at the rear spring hanger mounting, and the springs themselves were then mounted at their rear ends to a crossmember attached to the rear of the body. This curious arrangement had originally been thought out by Gordon Bashford as a way of getting round the limited rear wheel rebound movement of the underslung P1 chassis; if an upswept frame led to space reduction in the body, and an underslung frame gave suspension problems, then the obvious answer had to be no

A ¹⁄₁₆th scale model, dated July 1945, of a 'Proposed new saloon'. Despite the remarkably well-balanced styling, the proposal was never taken seriously, and seems not to have progressed to a full-size mock-up. Possibly Rover feared the cost of developing and tooling-up for such a radically new shape – or possibly they thought the British public was not ready for it!

The earliest full-size mock-ups of what was simply called a 'Proposed new car' date from November 1945. This spectacularly grotesque front end was built up on a prewar bodyshell which had simply been sawn down the middle and widened – the clay which disguised the join can just be seen.

By December 1945 the front end design had been tamed a little, although the horrible American-style bumpers are still in evidence. A contemporary note in the Rover archives confusingly describes this as 'P3'; exactly when P2 was cancelled and P3 began is not clear, as later mock-ups are described as 'model P' or, again, 'Proposed new car'.

Some sanity appeared to be returning by January 1946...

frame at all! Original ideas like this tended to go unnoticed in an era when the motoring public was less technically minded than it is now, but they do go to show just how much innovative thinking was being applied beneath the conventional exterior of Rover's cars.

Although the Girling independent front suspension was new to Rovers, it was basically similar to that which Lanchester had used on their Roadrider model in the 1930s. Rover had developed it to suit their own needs, first for the M-type economy car of 1945-46, which never got beyond the prototype stage, and now for the P3. It used lever-type hydraulic shock absorbers to form the top wishbone, set at an angle to lend the geometry a degree of anti-dive action, together with long radius arms at the bottom. It soon became apparent that the system gave poor control of small wheel movements, however, and George Mackie remembers removing front wings from test cars so that he could watch what was happening while someone else drove! For the 1949 season, a two-piece wishbone replaced the piston-type

...and this version was proposed in February. Only the grille, bumper and bumper valance details differ from the production P3.

Also proposed in February 1946 was this full-width front design.

dampers, and telescopic shock absorbers were fitted. At the same time, the radius arms were lengthened, and they now pivoted from the chassis crossmember which also supported the gearbox. Throughout P3 production, rubber bushes between suspension linkages and chassis were used to minimize noise transmission, and in conjunction with pre-packed bearings they helped reduce the need for lubrication to such an extent that the automatic chassis lubrication system of the P1s was no longer necessary.

The independent front suspension meant that it was no longer practicable to use rod-operated brakes, but Maurice Wilks had such faith in the Girling system that he retained as much of it as he could; thus the P3s had hydraulic front brakes linked to the familiar rod-operated brakes at the rear. This sort of compromise was typical of the era. Riley, for example, did the same for their first car with independent

front suspension – the RM series of 1946 – and Rolls-Royce used a system very similar to the Rover one, but modified to accept servo actuation. Hydro-mechanical brakes were not universally successful, the Riley version being prone to all kinds of troubles, while even the Rover brakes were markedly less efficient at low speeds than the all-mechanical system of the P1s. Rover proudly quoted a stopping distance of 30ft from 30mph with properly set-up mechanical brakes; the P3 took 38ft to stop from the same speed. Wheels of 17in diameter were standard, but 16in wheels could be specified, and the P3 had a new recirculating ball steering system by Burman incorporating a variable ratio for the first time on a Rover, which had the welcome benefit of reducing effort at parking speeds.

The P3's engine deserves consideration in some detail, because in one form or another it was to power Rover cars

Although this photograph is undated, it is generally thought to show another early postwar styling mock-up, despite the late 1930s wire wheels. Separate bonnet and wings are retained, but the nose has an unfamiliar shape, while the wings, running-boards and bumpers are new, and the boot lid treatment recalls the 1938-40 10hp Coupe.

The new engine, intended for the P2 but actually introduced in the P3, had overhead inlet and side exhaust valves with a sloping cylinder head. The P3 units breathed through a Solex carburettor.

The IOE layout of the P3 engine is clearly shown in this picture of a Rover display unit. The separate inlet manifold and head castings would be changed for the P4.

and Land-Rovers for over 30 years. The origins of the IOE design in the experimental V6 engine of the mid-1930s have already been discussed. The first in-line example was running before the war, and as soon as peacetime development work could begin again it was to the IOE layout that Maurice Wilks turned. A scaled-down four-cylinder IOE engine of 699cc was built to power the M-type prototypes in 1945, but the first production application was in 50bhp, 1,595cc four-cylinder form in the very first Land-Rovers of 1947. Perhaps the P3 application should really be considered as concurrent with the Land-Rover; after all, it was only the need to get the Land-Rover into production which held up the P3's introduction until

February 1948.

From a design point of view, the sloping-head inlet-over-exhaust layout was ideal for the time. The extremely efficient combustion chamber shape meant that there were no problems over using the low-grade Pool petrol which was then all that was available in Britain. In comparison with the '100mm' engine, the IOE unit was more flexible, its consumption of fuel was lower and it permitted quicker acceleration. It also promised quiet running for higher mileages, as a hydraulic timing chain tensioner prevented the familiar clatter of the high-mileage '100mm' engine from setting in; it was just as smooth, if not smoother, and it was extremely robust.

This interesting shot shows the P3's new front bumper and the pedestal-mounted pass lamp. GAC 915 was a pre-production vehicle and was first registered on October 2, 1947; it bears the grille badge of a 14hp.

Designed from the outset as an engine which could be produced in either four- or six-cylinder form, the IOE unit appeared as a 1,595cc 'four' and a 2,103cc 'six' of smaller bore in the P3s. RAC ratings would have been 11.98hp and 15.81hp, respectively (and the long stroke of the design was a reminder that it had been conceived under the RAC system of taxation), but the new cars were given model designations based on the engines' actual power output, doubtless because the RAC system ceased to apply to cars built after 1946. Thus what in P1 terms would have been a four-cylinder 12 became a 60, and what would have been a six-cylinder 16 became a 75. Both had a dual-downdraught Solex carburettor like those fitted to the six-cylinder P1s. Six 75s were made with a triple-SU installation, which endowed

the cars with much improved acceleration and a higher top speed than the standard model. The exact history of this variant remains obscure, although it has been said that the engines were experimental try-outs for the P4 75. Not that the standard cars were exactly sluggards; the 75 boasted a top speed of around 75mph, and the 60 could attain 72mph. In both cases, these speeds were reached more rapidly than by the equivalent 12s and 16s of 1947. It has already been seen that the two models used the same chassis; the shorter four-cylinder engine was simply set further back in the frame, giving the 60 rather less understeer than its six-cylinder cousin.

A look at production figures shows a drop of just over 2,000 cars for the first season of P3 production as compared

A four-light P3; by now, Rover had dropped the term Sports Saloon, although this particular example would certainly have been worthy of the name as its six-cylinder engine is fitted with triple carburettors.

to the final P1 season, and the 1949 season's total of 2,989 cars seems very low until one remembers that it represents the output for just over half a year, from January to August 1949. In fact, Solihull was working flat-out and total vehicle production had risen; the first Land-Rover was delivered in July 1948, and over 8,000 were built before the demise of the P3 in the autumn of 1949. Nevertheless, the P3 production total of 9,111 makes it the rarest of the classic Rovers.

Bodies
The P3 body panels were stamped out by Pressed Steel, but the bodies were assembled by Rover at Solihull. The range of styles was limited to two – although a handful of dropheads were also built – and it is interesting to note that the designation Sports Saloon had disappeared from the Company's literature. In its place was a four-light Saloon, as an alternative to the six-light Saloon, and a new pricing

policy meant that both bodies cost exactly the same on their respective chassis.

Although these bodies closely resembled the P1 Saloon and Sports Saloon, they actually shared very few common panels. The easiest way of seeing the difference is by comparing dimensions, when it becomes apparent that the P3 body was wider at the front and narrower at the back than its P1 counterpart. It also had less headroom and a slightly bigger boot. Overall, the 60 and 75 were shorter and wider than their predecessors, but the shorter wheelbase did not affect interior space as the P1 and P3 bodies were the same length. Twin horns and a pass lamp mounted on a central pillar ahead of the radiator helped to distinguish the new cars from their forebears at a quick glance.

Otherwise, there was little about P3 bodies worthy of comment. The facia arrangement and controls echoed P1 practice, the tool kit was still in a tray under the dashboard, and a sliding roof and louvres over the drop-glasses

The P3 readily recognizable from behind by its chrome overriders and wing-mounted tail lights. The extra width of the all-steel body was also easily seen in the larger rear window. Compare this picture of a six-light Saloon with the 1938 14hp shown on page 24.

continued to be provided. Improved ventilation with heater/demister ducting built into the bodyshell did away with the need for an opening windscreen, and a small Rover emblem filled the space in the dashboard where the opening handle had been on P1s. Now that the windscreen did not open there was no need for the off-screen wiper parking facility, and the independent control of the two wipers

disappeared. The main lighting switch moved from the dashboard to the left-hand side of the steering column and, following the practice of the final P1s, there was provision for the fitting of a radio in the dash; in some cases cars were factory-fitted with the Radiomobile Model 100 set. Probably the most noticeable interior difference from the P1s, however, was the use of plain leather seat facings in place of

The 1948 75 Graber Tourer, photographed when new. This car still survives in the hands of an enthusiast in the UK.

the more expensive ribbed type; not surprisingly, P3 seats were not as comfortable as their forebears.

In 1948, Rover arranged for a six-light 75 Saloon to be fitted by Tickford with a drophead coupe body similar to that concern's efforts on 1939-40 models. Although the car was shown on the Rover stand at the 1948 Motor Show, and two further examples were built later that year on specially-earmarked chassis, nothing further came of these experiments, the P4's arrival in autumn 1949 putting paid to any plans there may have been for production drophead bodies on the P3 chassis. Not surprisingly, the odd three-quarter chassis of the P3 did not attract the specialist coachbuilders and, indeed, Rover did not offer the car in chassis-only form. Nevertheless, in September 1948, Baumberger and Voster, the Swiss Rover agents, managed to obtain a right-hand-drive export chassis (number R8431157) on behalf of Herr Voster, who passed it to the coachbuilder Graber, in Zurich, and asked for a unique Tourer body to be built on it. A slab-sided body of semi-streamlined appearance (ultra-modern by contemporary standards) was duly built, and the car was shown on Graber's stand at the 1949 Geneva Motor Show. After a succession of owners, it came to Britain in 1962 and still exists, although it is not on the road at the time of writing. No other special-bodied P3s are known to have been built.

CHAPTER 4

The 'Auntie' Rover

Cyclops and successors, 1949 – 1964

P4 60 (1953-1959), **75** (1949-1959), **80** (1959-1962), **90** (1953-1959), **95** (1962-1964), **100** (1959-1962), **105** (1958-1959), **105R and 105S** (1956-1958), **110** (1962-1964)

The all-new postwar Rover finally materialized in 1949. Too late to affect the final shape of the P3, a new American car had been launched which in Maurice Wilks' view embodied the sort of proportions he could see as a Rover. As usual, he wanted a pattern to work from, and this time he found it in the 1947 Studebakers.

These Studebakers, in fact, had far-reaching effects on body design in the motor industry as a whole. Styled by the industrial designer Raymond Loewy in conjunction with Studebaker's Virgil Exner, they represented a new departure, in which bonnet, wings and body were no longer considered as separate entities; instead, there was a full-width bodyshell with slab sides from front to rear, and visual relief provided only by contour lines pressed into the panels. At the rear, the boot echoed and balanced the bonnet, to give what someone christened the 'going-both-ways' look. Maurice Wilks got his hands on one as soon as he could, and a 1948-model Studebaker Champion duly arrived at Solihull. Its body was stripped from its chassis and was fitted to the first P4 development chassis which, by a happy coincidence, shared the Studebaker's dimensions almost exactly. The so-called 'Roverbaker' ran as' a development vehicle for many years and was eventually rebuilt as a Studebaker again and used as a works hack.

Maurice Wilks set to work with Harry Loker to design the new Rover's body on the basis of the Studebaker. For the first time they used clay models instead of modifying full-size cars. The new body took shape, aping the 'going-both-ways' look and the four-light design of the Studebaker, but settling for rather less boxy styling and a pleasantly tapering boot line. The nose styling caused some headaches, as the garish grille of the Studebaker was clearly unsuitable and a traditional Rover grille was out of the question. One series of clay models had low-mounted headlamps behind perspex covers, but eventually the final full-size mock-up settled for a rather stark arrangement with the radiator grille's horizontal slats painted in the body colour and a Cyclopean pass lamp (carried over from the P3's separately-mounted lamp) recessed into the centre of the grille; head and side lamps were to be mounted in the wings. Thus the new car appeared in the autumn of 1949, its new and curious frontal aspect causing many a broken heart among devotees of the 'classic' Rover style exemplified by the P3s and the models of the later 1930s. The P4, however, was quite up-to-the-minute in styling; the delay had enabled Rover to base it on the 1947-season American fashion, while rivals like Standard, who had been quicker off the mark after the war, were stuck with models based on the outmoded 1942 style.

Chassis and engines

The P4's chassis was developed directly from that used in the P3 and was available in both left-hand and right-hand-drive form like its predecessor. Reasoning no doubt that the

Three different quarter-scale models were made for the P4, and were known as 500, 501 and 502, after the registration numbers painted on them. This is 500, which had an interesting chrome rubbing strip along the sides to match the bumpers. Headlamps are enclosed behind perspex covers, the grille design is odd, and a split windscreen is in evidence, but the general lines of the P4 are already there.

P4 production lines, *circa* 1950. The cars in this picture are later Cyclops model 75s, with the eight-bar grille.

The IOE engine and gearbox of a P4, pictured in 1953. This particular one was probably a development unit, as production examples did not have the curious plate visible here on the inlet manifold. The general appearance of the IOE engine remained unchanged throughout the P4's life, although there were variations in carburation, air cleaning arrangements, fan blades and, of course, the number of cylinders.

quality of postwar steel boded ill for the future of the P3s, with their rear springs mounted directly to the body, Gordon Bashford this time specified a full-length frame with the massive side-members gracefully upswept over the rear axle. The familiar semi-elliptic springs took care of the rear suspension, while the P3's IFS in its final form was retained at the front. Steering was once again Burman recirculating ball-type, although the six-cylinder P4s were always characterized by heavy understeer, the result of moving the engine forward in the frame to get more interior length than in the P3 within the same wheelbase.

In these essentials, the P4 chassis remained unchanged for the full 15 years of its production, and the major model differences were almost entirely related to the engines, which (very roughly) lent their power output figures as model designations. At first only one model was available, the 75, with 2,103cc six-cylinder engine. This differed from the P3 engine of the same capacity by its one-piece lightweight aluminium cylinder head and manifold, chromium-plated cylinder bores, and external oil filtration system through a Wipac filter mounted high up on the cylinder head. Twin SU carburettors with an oil-bath air cleaner replaced the dual-choke Solex of the P3, giving a slight increase in power, plus greater flexibility through increased torque.

The 75 was joined in autumn 1953 by the four-cylinder 60, one rung below it in the Rover hierarchy, and by the 90, a larger-engined 'six' one rung above. The requirement for 90bhp in this latter model, which was originally intended primarily for export, had led indirectly to a number of changes in the basic IOE engine design, because although the unit had been designed as a 'stretchable' one, the amount of over-boring necessary to extract the extra 15bhp

Rover liked to exhibit cutaway engines, and this photo shows a display version of the odd man out among P4 engines – the OHV 80 unit. The long transmission casing incorporates an overdrive.

led to siamesed bores. Rover built an experimental batch of 30 75s in 1950 with engines over-bored to 2,638cc, but the favoured customers to whom they went reported piston ring scuffing if the cars were driven really hard. So Joe Drinkwater, head of the Drawing Office's engine section, suggested that the cylinder bore centres could be repositioned within the block to leave more metal between each bore and thus give better cooling.

This 'spread bore' arrangement met with approval despite the additional complication of reducing the width of both big-end and main bearings as compared to the 75 engine. The production 'spread bore' engine consequently had bearings of tougher material than the 75's to cope with the increased unit loading. In six-cylinder 90 form, it developed 90bhp from 2,638cc, with an even lower compression ratio

than the 75's, which hinted that Rover might have a higher-performance version in mind for later. The 60 had 60bhp from a 1,997cc 'spread bore' engine with the same low compression ratio. Both engines used a single carburettor, the 60 breathing through a conventional oil-wetted gauze air cleaner, while the 90 (and export 60s) had a Vokes paper-element air cleaner; both had a rather more efficient oil filtration system than the 2,103cc engine. The 90's compression ratio was raised slightly in 1954, and then again in 1955 to give a 93bhp output, which the model would retain until its demise in 1959.

It obviously made sense to redesign the 75's engine along the same lines, and in the autumn of 1955 the 75 duly received its 'spread-bore' engine. Of slightly larger capacity than the earlier unit, this 2,230cc engine developed 80bhp (it

This picture, taken in August 1949, shows the first production P4 chassis. Note the massive side members and the rigid bracing of the frame. The P4 was the last production Rover car to have a separate chassis. In the background, the old guard is represented by a splendid Sports Saloon of the mid-1930s and a four-light P3.

The original P4 75 was a particularly handsome car. This photograph shows the central pass lamp, which earned it the nickname Cyclops.

is not clear why the model was not redesignated an 80) and gave much improved torque characteristics with a consequent increase in flexibility. Its single carburettor, breathing now through a Vokes paper-element air cleaner (although Export models, like 1956 Export 90s, had an oil-bath type), must have let Maurice Wilks and Jack Swaine sleep more easily, as experience with the original 75 had taught them that all the advantage of multiple-carburettor systems was lost if they were not regularly and competently tuned. That admitted, the next P4 engine was nevertheless to have twin carburettors!

The fourth and fifth P4 models arrived in autumn 1956, both using a twin-carburettor, high-compression version of the 90's engine which gave 108bhp. Oil-bath air cleaners had returned in January 1956 to Home Market 75s and 90s, and were fitted to the two 105 variants which, by virtue of their performance and fittings, immediately took over from the 90 at the top of the P4 range. If the 105S was quicker than the 90, however, it was also thirstier. Both the 105R and the 105S sold tolerably well for such expensive vehicles, but

The early P4s had a small rear window and a sloping boot lid. The circular reflectors on this 1950 Cyclops were added later, when red reflectors at the rear became a legal requirement. Photograph by Alan Milstead.

The Cyclops front end was discarded in 1952. This 1956 season 90 displays the replacement design, with the addition of the torpedo-style side lamps which had arrived in September 1954. 1952 and some 1953 models had chromed grille slats instead of the anodized aluminium type later standardized.

A larger boot, new tail lights and a three-piece wrap-around window arrived on 1955 season cars.

there is no doubt that the petrol rationing which followed the Suez crisis of 1957 did irreparable damage to their sales potential. The 105R was particularly badly affected, probably because its automatic transmission made it wasteful of fuel, and Rover dropped it from the range with something approaching relief when, in autumn 1958, the new P5 3-litre was able to offer an automatic option. The 105S became a 105 for 1959 and then disappeared altogether, along with its 60, 75 and 90 stablemates.

Inevitably, the arrival of the 3-litre had its effect on the existing saloon car range. One projected P4 model in the late 1950s had the 3-litre engine with Borg-Warner automatic transmission and power-assisted steering, but this disappeared from view when persistent trouble with camshafts and rockers in the existing P4 engines encouraged the Engineering Department to concentrate instead on developing a new 2.6-litre engine from the 3-litre unit, which used a

redesigned and more robust valve train. Once the P5 3-litre was available, the P4 assumed a new position as the 'cheaper' Rover, and there was obviously no point in having three six-cylinder cars as close in specification as the 75, 90 and 105 as second-string models. So for the 1960 season, the six-cylinder models were cut back to one, and the new 100 featured the 2,625cc engine which had been developed from the 3-litre unit. The latter was itself a development of the 'spread-bore' 90 engine with cylinder centres again repositioned, a seven-bearing crankshaft, and roller cam followers in place of the original pad type. Fitted with a single SU carburettor, the 100 engine was essentially a short-stroke 3-litre unit, with a power output of 104bhp. Once again, flexibility and torque had been improved, although – test results by the motoring journals notwithstanding – the 100 was not quite as quick as the superseded 105, even if it was marginally more frugal in its consumption of petrol.

The front end was changed again for 1957. This 90 well demonstrates the slightly bloated look of single-tone P4s of the era; two-tone cars had a trim strip dividing the colours after autumn 1957, and this was later standardized as a way of slimming down the styling.

Also introduced in the autumn of 1959 was the 80, a four-cylinder replacement for the 60. It was the only P4 not to use a variant of the IOE engine, having instead a 2,286cc OHV engine similar to that in the contemporary Land-Rover and developed from the Land-Rover's 2,052cc diesel unit. In cubic capacity, this engine was actually larger than that of the six-cylinder 75, so to some extent the 80 may also be said to have replaced the cheapest of the superseded six-cylinder range. Developing 77bhp and fitted with a Solex carburettor breathing through the by now customary oil-bath air cleaner, the OHV unit made the 80 slightly quicker than the 60 it replaced, but the Land-Rover engine did betray some of its agricultural origins and there was a problem with timing-chain noise in the earlier examples. Nevertheless, the four-cylinder engine was mounted further back in the chassis than the 'sixes', with the result that the 80 suffered less from the characteristic P4 understeer.

The 80 and 100 were christened 'Mk IV' models when the new chassis numbering system arrived in June 1961 (although no-one seems to know why). Both survived until autumn 1962, when they were replaced by two new six-cylinder models based on the 100, which were destined to be the last P4s of all. With impeccable logic, these were known as 'Mk I' models! The 95's engine was identical to that of the 100 except for a valve timing revision which put power down to 102bhp and enabled use of a higher axle ratio, while the new 110 was fitted with the redesigned cylinder head and inlet manifold which had been developed for the 3-litre, and with that car's larger carburettor and paper-element air cleaner. Since 1949, the IOE engines had had a lightweight one-piece head and manifold casting, which was relatively cheap to produce but permitted little tuning. By using separate castings for head and manifold, Rover found they were able to cast more efficient shapes for the inlet manifold tracts. The inlet port shape was reworked by performance development expert Harry Weslake, and the resulting so-called 'Weslake head' gave the 110's engine a maximum power output of 123bhp, the highest of all the P4s. The 110's acceleration was consequently quite as good as that of the twin-carburettor 105 and 105S, and its claimed

This 100 shows the later style of two-tone paint, and the new hubcaps with dished centres which came in with the disc-braked cars. The recessed front grille and new bumpers had been introduced in 1958 to give the P4 closer visual links with the P5 3-litre.

top speed of nearly 106mph made it the fastest P4 of all in that respect. Sadly, it was also the thirstiest.

The very first 75s had a hydro-mechanical braking system similar to that of the P3, but with twin leading shoes instead of leading-and-trailing shoes at the front. From autumn 1950 a fully hydraulic all-drum system was standard, which from the 1956 season was improved by the use of shorter linings designed to prevent grabbing or knocking while reversing. The 1956-59 90s, and all 105 variants, had twin trailing shoes at the front. Servo assistance arrived for the 1956 season, but was initially confined to overdrive-equipped 90s because Solihull reasoned that if the engine stalled on a freewheeling servo-equipped car, a panic-stricken driver might exhaust the servo and find himself with neither brakes nor engine braking. The servo was standard on the 105R and 105S models, and remained so until the demise of the 105 in 1959. After autumn 1959, all models had servo-assisted brakes as standard, with Girling discs on the front wheels in place of the original drums. Disc-braked cars had dished wheel rims so that the wheels should not protrude

beyond the bodywork; in order to maintain the same track, this meant that the rear axle had to be widened slightly. The disc-braked cars could be specified with wider 6.40-section tyres instead of the 6.00-section tyres which remained standard until the end of P4 production. These fatter tyres, still on the 15in wheels which the P4 had always used, tended to make the steering heavier at parking speeds, and a lower steering box ratio was standardized in autumn 1960 to redress the balance.

One of the P4's more endearing idiosyncrasies was its handbrake. Sited outboard and ahead of the driver so that a bench front seat could be fitted, it was initially the subject of complaint from customers who found that they could not reach it. Rover added a rearward extension during the 1950 season, giving the lever its famous 'shepherd's crook' configuration, and then had second thoughts for 1954, specifying a pull-up lever positioned between the driver's seat and the door. This seems to have met with considerable market resistance, with the result that the 'shepherd's crook' was reinstated for 1955 and, after a further small

A 1959 75, showing the extra chrome added over the rear number-plate for that season.

much to be desired in comparison with the gear change of P3 and earlier Rovers, and its sobriquet of 'pot-stirrer' is adequately descriptive! The long, cranked handle was so designed in order to leave legroom for a third passenger on the bench front seat; certainly not made for fast changing, it was nevertheless adjustable to suit the driver's reach, and Rover never changed it until the end, even employing the same design on the first P5 3-litre cars.

The P4 gearbox was essentially that of the P3, with a raised third gear ratio to give better acceleration. Synchromesh covered third and fourth gears only until autumn 1953, when it was added to second as well, but it was never extended to first. Prior to the arrival of the 80 and 100 models in autumn 1959, gearboxes featured the Rover freewheel, except that Laycock DeNormanville overdrive was optionally available instead on the 90 from autumn 1955, on the 60 and 75 from the following year, and was standard on the 105S/105 models. Both 80 and 100 models

This magnificent 1964 110 was overall prizewinner at the 1982 Rover P4 Drivers' Guild's National Concours. The 110 was the only P4 to have the later 3-litre type wheel covers.

modification for 1956, remained unchanged until the end of production.

Gear levers were also below previous Rover standards on the P4. Instead of the tidy floor-mounted lever of the P3s, the first P4s had an American-style column change, which was woolly in the extreme. It was far from universally appreciated, and a floor-change conversion was offered by Gethin's, the Rover distributors in Birmingham. This conversion, which was found particularly on Police models but was otherwise rare, seems to have been brought to Gethin's by Peter Wilks, one of the progenitors of the P4 75-based Marauder sports car, which had an almost identical gear change.

The purpose of the column change was of course also to make room for the bench front seat, but Rover finally gave in to customer pressure and fitted a new floor-mounted gear lever for the 1954 season, coinciding with the introduction of the 60 and 90 models. It has to be said that this still left

An unusual shot, taken in June 1949, of a P4 prototype without its doors. The plain leather seat facings and generous leg room all round are well illustrated. Note the angular overriders, which differed from the production items, the 15-bar grille and the extra chrome around headlights and air intakes.

had overdrive as standard (although it was only standardized at the very last moment, and a small number of early cars were built without it, having a four-speed gearbox with no freewheel) and all 110 models had overdrive. For those who wanted better acceleration and more relaxed cruising, a high 3.9:1 axle ratio was introduced in 1955 as an option for the non-overdrive 90, and was actually more common than is generally supposed. The 3.9 axle returned on the 95, the only manual-transmission model offered with neither overdrive nor freewheel.

Various semi-automatic and preselector gearboxes had been available in Britain since the 1930s, and indeed Rover's own freewheel could be seen as a form of semi-automatic in that it offered clutchless gear changing. By the mid-1950s, however, fully automatic transmissions were just beginning to catch on in the upper regions of the UK market; Rolls-Royce, for example, had introduced theirs in 1954. Rover decided to follow this American-inspired trend, linking an automatic gearbox to the torquiest of the P4 engines in the 105R. They preferred to design and build

their own automatic gearbox rather than use an expensive imported unit, and the Roverdrive transmission fitted to the 105R is a fascinating representative of Britain's home-grown answers to the American automatic gearboxes. Unfortunately, Rover were not able to install it without incurring a cost penalty; their transmission was so long that the 105R had to have special chassis alterations to accommodate it!

Like modern automatic transmissions, the Roverdrive had a torque convertor behind the flywheel, but this used oil from the sump. Behind it was a servo-operated single-dry-plate clutch, a two-speed-and-reverse manual gearbox, and then an overdrive set to cut in automatically. Normally, the car would start in 'Intermediate' (the top gear of the main box) and the overdrive would take over at higher speeds; a manual override gave selection of 'Emergency Low', or the bottom gear of the synchromesh box, to give more torque for climbing steep hills or more engine braking for descending them. The Roverdrive unit was long-lived and generally reliable; its main problem was that it endowed the 108bhp 105R with acceleration little better than the

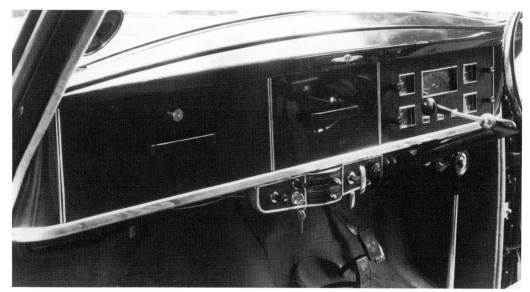

An interior view of an early Cyclops. The rectangular instruments disappeared after a single season, and an extension was added to the handbrake lever even before that, but the column gear change would remain until 1953.

considerably cheaper 60bhp 60 model. It was not universally liked at Solihull, either; Jack Swaine scornfully dismisses its acceleration as 'pathetic'. Nevertheless, as the first ever automatic Rover, it holds a special place in the Company's history.

Bodies

The basic shape of the P4 body, and in particular its passenger cabin, did not alter between 1949 and 1964, so that a 'Cyclops' is instantly recognizable as the elder sister of a 95 or 110. All the shells were built by Pressed Steel at Cowley, originally with door, bonnet and boot lid panels of Birmabright aluminium alloy. As introduced in the autumn of 1949, the P4 75 had the 'Cyclops' nose, featuring a 15-bar radiator grille and chrome trimming around the headlamps and air intake grilles. This chrome trimming rapidly disappeared, and the 15-bar grille went out in favour of a similar one with only eight bars after overheating problems showed up. From behind, these early cars were distinguished by a small oval window similar to that of the P3,

horizontal tail lamps, and a sloping boot lid with a square number-plate box and a large vertical handle. A look inside revealed a bench seat at the front and a full-width dashboard with rectangular instruments ahead of the driver. The stalk switches on the steering column for lights and indicators were new to Rovers, and the bench front seat had brought with it that American-style column gear change and the handbrake lever displaced to somewhere by the driver's right knee (or left knee on LHD cars). The semi-circular horn ring on the steering wheel was American in origin, too. Both outside and inside the car there were new pushbutton door handles, those inside doubling as door pulls, but the polished walnut dashboard and door cappings, the deep pile carpets, and of course the leather seats, were all in the familiar Rover mould, although the plain seat facings of the P3 had been retained.

By the standards of the day, the 75 was a very well-equipped car, but Rover offered a number of optional extras. Owners could specify additional wheel trim rings ('rimbellishers'), a badge bar mounted between the over-

Pleated leather first appeared for the 1956 season. A bench front seat is fitted to this car, although individual seats had also become available. The circular instrument faces had arrived in 1950 and the 'pot-stirrer' gear lever in 1953.

riders, and a windscreen washer kit. Louder windtone horns were available and the passenger compartment could be furnished with footrests for the rear, floor mats, a cigarette lighter and either felt or plastic seat covers.

Even so, Solihull did not get the new style right first time. As already noted, the handbrake lever had to be modified during the 1950 season, and the rectangular instruments were also not well-received, so that circular dials replaced them from autumn 1950. At the same time, the clock moved to the centre of the wooden facia rail. In addition, the doors gained rising hinges, orthodox interior handles in place of the pushbutton type, and their courtesy lights were rewired to operate independently of the side lamps.

A number of radical revisions were introduced in March 1952. Most immediately apparent was a new front end, with a chromed grille bearing a triangular badge similar to that of

the P3s. The 'Cyclops' pass lamp had disappeared, and instead there were Lucas double-dipping headlamps to suit the new lighting regulations. The wing area around these lamps had been tidied up, and there was also a new valance between bumper and body. This new front end, which had really been necessitated by customer resistance to the original pattern, had also permitted a change in the heating and ventilating arrangements. The air intake was now mounted high up on the scuttle, where it would no longer pick up fumes and dust from the road, and was covered by a flap controlled from the dashboard. At the same time, the opportunity had been taken to fit a more powerful heater.

Small changes had also occurred at the rear; the rear window was wider and the number-plate box was rectangular, the overall result being that the car looked wider and lower from behind. The spare wheel was now accessible through a flap beneath the bumper, and the rear body mountings had been changed relative to the chassis so that there was an extra inch of headroom for back seat passengers. The seats themselves had improved springing, and a recess in the front seat back increased legroom for those behind. The driver's job was made easier by a more controllable organ-type accelerator pedal and self-parking windscreen wipers, while there was a new circular horn ring, and the low-fuel warning light was replaced by a reserve tap. In addition, there were changes to the lighting and freewheel controls.

Two-tone paint schemes put in their first appearance during 1953, but were limited to two; there was dark grey over light grey or dark green over light green, the upper colour covering the roof panel only. With the introduction of the 60 and 90 models for 1954 came a handbrake repositioned between the driver's seat and the door. The handy door pockets were deleted so that the driver's should not foul the new handbrake, and chromed interior door pull handles arrived a few months later in March 1954. The 90 models were distinguished by a fog lamp mounted on the left-hand side of the front bumper, and by 'Rover 90' in elegant script on the bonnet sides and boot lid. Grille badges, of course, bore the appropriate model designation – 60, 75, or 90.

In the meantime, Maurice Wilks had realized that Rover needed a professional body stylist. It was all very well starting from the basis of another car and adapting the design to suit a Rover, but it was a process which could not continue indefinitely. In late 1953, Wilks took on David Bache, who had served his apprenticeship with Austin at Longbridge, with the intention of grooming him as Rover's stylist. At this time, thoughts were beginning to turn to new models at Solihull, and Bache prepared some new designs for Wilks' approval. Although there were those at Rover who were highly impressed, Bache recalls that Maurice Wilks was horrified, and reminded him that while these designs were very good, Rovers were supposed to be discreet, not eye-catching! It was quite clear that a P4 was going to have to look like a P4 for some time to come, and indeed Bache was only ever allowed to make subtle revisions

to update the body styling in subsequent years.

For the 1955 season he was able to give the P4 bodies a raised boot line and consequent increase in luggage space, along with a much wider wrap-around rear window, divided into three sections, no doubt because Maurice Wilks had reservations about the strength of large areas of curved glass. Flashing trafficators were now beginning to replace semaphore arms, and recent legislation demanded red reflectors at the rear, so Bache killed two birds with one stone by combining trafficators, tail lights and reflectors in new vertical clusters at the rear. He gave the old front side lamps larger lenses and made them trafficators, while the side lamps emerged on top of the wings in chromed housings. Together with these changes came a widening of the two-tone paint options, better door sealing, and the provision of body touch-up pencils in the tool tray. The handbrake returned to its former position after attracting unfavourable comment in its 1954 location, and the door pockets were reinstated, although the economy-model 60 kept its pocketless door panels.

1956-season changes focussed on the interior, where pleated seat coverings and optional individual front seats were finally introduced, the former having been absent from Rovers since the arrival of the P3 in 1948. Apart from a change from clear to amber front indicator lenses, external revisions had to wait until the 1957 season, when a tidier front wing design by David Bache represented the first of a series of revisions intended to stress the family resemblance between the P4 and the as yet unreleased P5 3-litre. Meanwhile, the 90 lost its distinguishing fog lamp, and the new 105S and 105R De Luxe were fitted with twin fog lamps. These latter models both had rimbellishers and a cigar lighter as standard. Many 105R De Luxe models also had the optional rear footrests, which were otherwise rare, and this probably reflects the car's attraction as a chauffeur-driven vehicle.

All three 105 models had bonnet and boot lid badging in a rather less attractive script than the 90's, and there were, of course, distinguishing grille badges, that of the 105R being in yellow-and-brown instead of the red-and-black traditional to Rovers since 1930. The new models had plastic grille

The dashboard of a 105R, showing the unusual gear selector lever. Pressing the button in the knob activated the servo-operated clutch.

At the end, the P4 came to share the 3-litre's seat design. These non-reclining seats are on an 80, 95 or 100, but fully reclining seats of the same pattern were available on 110s and the later 95s.

badges, and the enamel badges of the older models were gradually phased out in favour of plastic ones, beginning in 1957 with the 90. Inside, the recessed door pockets fitted since 1954 to the 75 and 90 were replaced by flat pockets, which were also added to the 60 and found on the 105R and 105S models.

P4 changes for the 1958 season were limited in number, and to some extent were intended to pave the way for the 3-litre. The seats were given padded rolls at the edges, covered with plain leather, which greatly improved passenger location when cornering, and there was a revised gear selector quadrant for the 105R, with a rubber mat on the car's gearbox cover to resist the wear caused by the driver's idle left foot. The wool headlining was replaced in January 1958 by a washable plastic one available in only two colours. Outside, changes clearly envisaged earlier were introduced, and the two-tone colour scheme now divided along the top of the wings, giving a greater area for the upper colour. A chromed dividing strip was added, which became optional on the single-colour cars as well after December 1957. The 60 now received its plastic grille badge, leaving only the 75 with the earlier enamel variety.

The P5 3-litre was introduced in the autumn of 1958, and P4 models for 1959 were given the final stage of their facelift to underline the family resemblance. New bumpers and overriders, together with a recessed radiator grille and new-style 'Rover' nameplate, all followed the P5 pattern. A chromed embellisher above the rear number-plate again echoed the P5 design, and had the useful benefit of making the cars appear lower and wider from behind. All models now had the chrome side trim strip as standard, and an interior revision added a padded roll to the dashboard top, partly in a reflection of the 3-litre design, but also to some extent for safety reasons. The 105 could be distinguished from its 105S predecessor both by new badging and by the absence of that model's twin fog lamps and rimbellishers; inside, it had also lost the cigar lighter.

From the time of the appearance in autumn 1959 of the 80 and 100 models, P4 bodies changed very little indeed, and then only in badging and interior details. The 100 had script badging on its bonnet and boot lid, while the 80 had only its grille badge as identification. Both models had a key-operated starter switch in place of the pushbutton type, but otherwise changes from previous models were confined to small details such as the provision of interior coat hooks and the arrival in autumn 1961 of twin ashtrays instead of the single central type in the back of the front bench seats. These cars had 3-litre style recessed-centre hubcaps, and a new type of badge bar was introduced for them because the old type could not be fitted with the post-1958 overriders.

More major changes had to wait until 1962, when the 95 and 110 models shared with the revised P5 3-litres larger, clearer instrument dials with black instead of chrome bezels, spade-shaped switches, and instrument voltage stabilization. The 110 had rear arm slings and was available optionally with reclining individual front seats. Identification of both models was by chrome script badges in the usual places, although grille badges came from the 3-litre and consequently bore no model number. The 95 also had recessed-centre hubcaps, while the 110 had the larger wheel covers introduced on the 3-litre in 1961.

Crushable sun visors replaced the translucent plastic type during the 1963 season, and a picnic table made by an accessory manufacturer was offered as a new optional extra. It fitted over the gearbox cover, and remained rare. From March 1963, the Birmabright alloy body panels were replaced by heavier steel panels for reasons which have never been satisfactorily explained (perhaps it was more important to divert the supplies of alloy to the P6, which had both bonnet and boot lid of this material). Final detail changes came in the 1964 season, when both models received the cold-start switch of the 3-litre, and reclining seats became an option for the 95. Rover also approved a Webasto fabric sunroof for that season, and a number of 95s and 110s were so fitted.

Experiments and prototypes

Although the production P4s never wavered from the stolid four-light body which earned them their nickname of 'Auntie' – they represented the same staid respectability in the 1950s as did 'Auntie' BBC – Solihull was not short of alternative ideas. As early as 1950-51, a two-door drophead version was under consideration, and the two prototypes built by Salmons-Tickford, who of course had supplied the prewar drophead bodies, looked uncommonly like the gas turbine car JET 1. This car, described later, may well have been the source of inspiration. No-one at Rover seems to know why these elegant three-position dropheads never went into production. Next on the experimental list may have been a fixed-head coupe model, although it is possible that the contemporary witness who described this car as 'short' and 'round-backed' in fact confused it with a proposed Road Rover design on the P4 chassis.

The best-known of the proposed alternative body styles for the P4, however, is that designed in 1953 by Farina. The Turin concern was approached by the Rover Company some time late in 1952, and crafted a beautiful two-door drophead body for the P4 in the typical contemporary Italian idiom. This was fitted to a 75 chassis, and a fixed-head version was built shortly afterwards and fitted to a 90 chassis. The

Known at Solihull as the Rover Coupe, this is one of two prototype dropheads based on Cyclops 75s which were constructed in 1950-51 by Salmons-Tickford. They had two doors in place of the standard car's four, special pleated leather seat coverings and a split-squab arrangment at the front to permit rear access. At least one still survives, but in a very dilapidated condition.

The Farina drophead was attractively finished in metallic gold with a red convertible top. It still exists, albeit in rebuilt form, in the hands of an enthusiast.

Farina's fixed-head coupe on the P4 90 chassis served as the starting-point for P5 styling. The car was eventually sold to a Rover concessionaire in Spain, and is thought to have been written off in an accident.

drophead was shown on the Rover stand at the 1953 London Motor Show with the intention of gauging public reaction. Considerable interest was shown, and Rover commissioned a copy of the car (probably just the one, although a persistent rumour suggests two) from the Mulliner Coachbuilding Company in Birmingham. Sadly, this showed that production costs would be far too high, and the project was cancelled. Nevertheless, the Farina bodies were the underlying inspiration when Maurice Wilks tasked David Bache with designing the body for the P5 3-litre.

After that, Rover fought shy of special bodies, probably as much because space at Solihull was limited after the runaway success of the Land-Rover as because they feared the concomitant high costs. Nevertheless, the story is told of one other P4 drophead of the mid-1950s, supposedly built by Graber, in Switzerland, and evaluated at Solihull sometime around 1957. An eye-witness describes it as a dark green car which resembled Graber's design for the contemporary Alvis, but no further traces have yet been found. As for estate cars, Rover do not seem to have considered the P4 suitable for conversion (it was high and narrow, which would have handicapped it against contemporaries like the Humber estates), although at least one estate car was built in

1960 on a P4 100 chassis, allegedly by apprentices at Solihull. This car had a wooden-framed rear body, similar in construction to that of the Morris Minor Traveller.

Of course, the P4 was used extensively as a testbed for other components. In the early 1950s, the V6 engine proposed for the P5 was road-tested in a series of P4s, although none were made available to the public. At least one P4 was fitted in the later 1950s with a Land-Rover diesel engine (initially 2,052cc, later 2,286cc), and opposing views from the Experimental Department say it was either for mileage testing or in prospect of an order for diesel P4 taxis from Brazil, which was never fulfilled because Solihull could not refine the engines sufficiently to meet their own high standards! There were also two very special vehicles based on P4s which were run by Gordon Bashford's Advanced Engineering team in the mid-1950s. One was built up as a monocoque structure in order to test P5 construction methods and had an experimental double-wishbone front suspension, while the second and later one was built up as a

This wooden-bodied estate car on a P4 100 chassis, photographed by Jim Ritson, still survives.

60

base unit, P6-fashion.

Last, but by no means least, the P4 formed the basis of Rover's experiments with gas turbine propulsion for road vehicles in the early 1950s. Once the Company's experiments in the early postwar period had resulted in the design of a gas turbine engine which appeared suitable for automobile use, Gordon Bashford was given the job of building the car into which to fit it. Rather than start from scratch with a new and expensive design, he simply adapted a P4 'Cyclops'. The gas turbine engine, too bulky for the P4's engine compartment, was installed amidships behind the front seats. This automatically reduced the car to a two/three-seater, so Bashford cut the roof off and welded up the back doors to make an attractive and streamlined tourer-type body. There was no hood stowage space, so the car had no hood. As originally built, it had a rather upright windscreen, but twin aero screens were substituted later, probably for effect as much as for better aerodynamics. XT1 (Experimental Turbine number 1) is more familiarly known by the name of JET 1, the registration number which the Rover

The third gas turbine car was T2A, with its engine mounted at the rear. The vast exhaust funnel meant that the rear window had to be widened; there were also twin bumpers (purpose unexplained) and an extra air intake ahead of the windscreen. Someone had dented the front passenger door by the time this picture was taken!

Company obtained for it.

After preliminary proving trials before the RAC's Technical Committee in March 1950, at which the world's first turbine car earned its makers the RAC's Dewar Trophy, JET 1 went back to Solihull for further engine development work. It resurfaced over two years later with more power and a new bumperless nose based on the then-current P4 grille, but with Marauder-like front wings. The gas turbine team took it to Belgium, and on June 25, 1952, Spen King achieved a maximum speed of 152.196mph in the car on the sealed-off Jabbeke Highway. More might possibly have been achieved, but as this record-breaking stunt was really for publicity purposes, Rover thought it more profitable to devote the available cash to more practical in-car development work.

A 'more practical' gas turbine car actually existed already. T2, with a much smaller and less powerful power unit installed orthodox-fashion at the front, had already been made from a P4 75 saloon. However, the tremendously hot exhaust gases of the gas turbine engine caused problems; Rover tried to duct them through the chassis side-members, but only extensive and impractical lagging was able to

An unfamiliar shot of JET 1 as first completed, with a conventional windscreen in place of the aero screens with which it was usually seen. Standing behind the car from left to right are Maurice Wilks, Spencer Wilks and Frank Bell, who headed Rover's early gas turbine team.

counter the car's consequent tendency to self-ignite! As a result, T2 was rebuilt as T2A, still under Gordon Bashford's supervision, sometime around 1954. This time the engine went into the boot, and a huge funnel running up to roof height took away the exhaust gases, as well as most of the rearward visibility. It is not quite clear why nothing further came of T2A, although the next gas turbine car, T3, was designed around its power unit, so it may be that the P4 was felt to have reached the limit of its potential as a gas turbine-driven vehicle.

The Marauder

No P4 history would be complete without at least a brief look at the Marauder. This two/three-seat sports tourer depended entirely on P4 75 components for its chassis, engine and transmission (although a special overdrive was optionally available, several years before the P4 90 became so equipped), and it depended to no small degree on the same car for its styling. Nevertheless, it was not a Rover product, but was assembled by Wilks, Mackie and Company (later known as the Marauder Car Company) from P4 mechanical parts, and clothed with a body of special design. Between 1950 and the middle of 1952, when increased Purchase Tax priced the Marauder out of the market, 15 were made.

The car was designed by Peter Wilks, George Mackie and Spen King, all Rover employees, with assistance in the styling from Richard Mead, a small Midlands coachbuilder. Their original plan had been to use Rover parts in a traditional cycle-winged open sports car, but the appearance of the Ferrari 166 in 1949 encouraged them to give the car wide-bodied styling based on the P4. A supply of parts from Rover was arranged, Wilks and Mackie left the Rover Company to set up in business making Marauders – though both would later return to Solihull – and the first prototype appeared in July 1950.

Basically, the Marauder used a shortened P4 chassis

Magnificently restored by one of its original designers, George Mackie's Marauder is seen here in 1981. The general resemblance to the P4 body design is clearly seen – and what about those hubcaps and bumpers, and the trim strip at the base of the body!

frame, with a slightly uprated 2,103cc engine mounted further back than in the parent car to avoid its heavy understeer and to give a more appropriate weight distribution. Later, an over-bored engine of 2,390cc, using pistons from the P3 60 and giving 100bhp, would be offered in the Marauder 100, and it would be possible to specify a triple-carburettor option with the larger engine. Only one car of each type was actually built, however.

Marauders were good for around 90mph in basic form, and rather more in '100' form – not exactly road-burners, but certainly sporting and refined for cars of their type. In the early 1950s they established a name for themselves in rallies and even club racing events. A single example was fitted with a rather less sporting fixed-head coupe body to special order, and this, along with at least 10 other Marauders, still survives.

CHAPTER 5

A move up-market

The P5 programme, 1958 – 1973

P5 3-litre (1958-1967), P5B 3.5-litre (1967-1973), P5 2.4-litre (1962) and 2.6-litre (1962-1966)

In the early 1950s, Rover's finances favoured an expansion of the model range, and the Company at first toyed with the idea of producing a smaller car than the P4 alongside that model. It soon became clear that neither the capital nor the production facilities then available would stretch to the volume production necessary for such a car, however, and in 1955 a plan was approved to make the new model a bigger car than the P4, a 3-litre luxury saloon which would be produced in relatively small numbers. It would also take Rover into a higher price bracket than they had previously catered for under the Wilks regime.

In common with many other manufacturers, Rover had been experimenting in the early 1950s with monocoque structures, and it was swiftly decided in conjunction with the body stylists that this type of construction offered the opportunity for reducing body height in the search for sleeker lines and better handling without a corresponding loss of interior space. Thus the P5 was drawn up as a monocoque design, with the engine, transmission and front suspension carried on a detachable subframe. Like all the early monocoque cars, it was over-engineered by the time it went into production; stress engineering was then in its infancy, and the solution to all doubts about structural strength was to make the doubtful components thicker! The subframe ended up like a massive part-chassis, and an early experiment with Birmabright alloy body panels was soon aborted in favour of the heavier all-steel construction. It was

thus no mean achievement that the car's overall weight was closely similar to that of the contemporary six-cylinder P4s.

Mechanical units

The choice of a 3-litre engine was dictated by the minimum size then considered acceptable in a luxury car rather than for any deeper engineering reasons. A lot of work went into a V6 unit distantly related to the prewar V6 which Jack Swaine had drawn up, but the engine's development was beset by problems, and by late 1955 or early 1956 it had become clear that the V6 could not possibly be ready in time for the P5's projected launch date of 1958. Maurice Wilks instructed Swaine's department to stop work on the engine (which at that stage gave around 100bhp from 2,960cc and was running in several P4 development cars) and to look into the possibility of making a 3-litre unit from the 2,638cc P4 90 block.

It would have been possible simply to over-bore the 90's block and to fit the pistons from a 60, but Swaine's team had lingering doubts about the engine's durability with the resultant thin cylinder walls, so Maurice Wilks revised the requirement, asking for a block of the same dimensions, but with water between all the bores. He also specified a seven-bearing crankshaft (could it have been coincidence that the XK engine in Jaguar's Mk VII saloon already boasted seven main bearings?) to ensure vibration-free running. Norman Bryden, in the Engine Drawing Office, came up with the simple solution of repositioning the cylinder bore centres within the block, as had already been

One of David Bache's earliest proposals for the P5 was this rather chunky-looking machine. Note the rear window design, which had already appeared on the P4.

Viewing of this full-scale mock-up took place on a Sunday morning at Solihull in late 1955. The design now had links with the Farina P4 prototypes, but the wheelbase at this stage was only 108in.

This view of an early P5 Saloon bodyshell shows the massively robust construction.

done once for the 'spread bore' engine, and was able to ensure that the only increase in length was a tiny one, brought about because the water pump impeller now had to move forwards to clear No 1 cylinder barrel. Time and money were saved by using a cylinder head which, as Jack Swaine recalls, was a compromise based on that of the 90. Improved valve gear used roller cam followers (first seen in the 2-litre Land-Rover diesel engine) in place of the pad type, which tended to wear rapidly in the P4 engine; there were a new camshaft, distributor and exhaust manifold, a higher compression ratio and a bigger carburettor, and the 3-litre engine was complete.

From its introduction in the autumn of 1958 until the demise of the Mk IA 3-litre in 1962, the 2,995cc engine developed 115bhp at 4,500rpm. Although this was not significantly more than the 108bhp twin-caburettor P4 engine installed in the 105 models, the torque characteristics of the new engine gave it much greater flexibility over a wider range. Thus the P5 3-litre offered a smoother, more relaxed manner of motoring, as befitted a high-quality

luxury saloon. It was scarcely a quick car, however, and proposals at Board level for 'economy model' P5s – first with a 2-litre 'four' and later with the 2,625cc 'six' – were accordingly given short shrift. The Engineering Department, meanwhile, tried to coax more power from the 3-litre engine by means of various multiple-carburettor systems. The car's relative lack of urge did not go unnoticed outside the Rover Company, either – although, surprisingly, the motoring press never complained in print – and the former racing driver Raymond Mays developed a triple-carburettor installation which he intended to market. Tests made at Solihull, however, showed that the advantages of this installation were minimal, and Mays never actually put his conversion into production.

The Mk I 3-litre engine, produced from 1958 until 1961, used an oil-bath air cleaner, but this was replaced on the 1962 season Mk IA models by an AC paper-element cleaner. This offered easier maintenance and may also have been intended to contribute to better breathing, although the Mk IA engines showed no noticeable power increase over the

The P5 subframe, complete with engine, transmission and front suspension. The rear ends of the subframe side members bolted to the monocoque shell approximately under the front seats. This is an early example, with the original drum brakes.

Mk I variety. Restricted breathing had actually been identified quite early on as the main cause of the 3-litre's lack of power. After the multiple-carburettor experiments, Maurice Wilks asked for simpler ways of improving the engine's breathing, and the engine development team eventually came up with the so-called 'Weslake head', which has already been described in Chapter 4.

Solihull's original plan had been to fit a high-performance version of the 3-litre engine to the forthcoming Coupe models, but in the event, the 'Weslake head' engine was fitted to both Saloon and Coupe Mk II 3-litre models in autumn 1962. As fitted to manual-transmission cars, it offered 134bhp and a slight increase in maximum torque,

both at higher crankshaft speeds than in the Mk I version. A lower-compression version with other minor differences and developing 129bhp was fitted to automatic cars, as their transmission required different torque characteristics, and a less tortuous exhaust system on both manual and automatic Mk II models released a little more of this new-found power to the road wheels. If the automatics were still rather deficient in acceleration, they could at least top the 100mph mark without difficulty, and the manual transmission Mk IIs could boast a performance worthy of such a large engine. By this time, however, the rather sedate market into which the 3-litre had been launched was beginning to change, and there were signs that many customers at the top end of the market were now prepared to sacrifice a little luxury for a lot more performance. Although the car continued to sell well, it never repeated the sales success of its first years, and settled down as a steady seller in a rapidly shrinking market.

From autumn 1964, the 3-litre engine was given larger main bearing journals to counteract a torsional vibration of the crankshaft which Solihull's engineers had encountered with the 'Weslake head' engine. No normal owner would ever have detected this, but the story does demonstrate how much attention to detail went into Rover development! Cars fitted with this engine were designated Mk IIC models. The same engine, with its accompanying larger-capacity cooling system, also powered the facelifted Mk III models introduced for the 1966 season, when a change in the type of automatic transmission led to the 134bhp engine being fitted to automatic as well as manual-gearbox Mk IIIs, but otherwise there were no major changes of specification.

With the introduction of the 3.5-litre model in 1967, Rover were at last able to provide the sort of performance which the luxury market was by now demanding. By this stage, of course, the car's body design was beginning to date, but that seems to have worked in its favour, allowing the new model to carve out a niche in the market which was all its own. The 3.5-litre was powered by a lightweight all-alloy 3,528cc V8 engine which had been developed from a General Motors design, and was related to the engines with which Jack Brabham and his team had won world motor racing titles in 1966 and 1967.

The story of the V8 has been told many times, but bears repetition. Managing Director William Martin-Hurst spotted one of the GM engines in 1963 while on a visit to Mercury Marine, at Fond du Lac, Wisconsin, to sell Rover engines for marine applications. On inquiring of that company's Carl Keikhaefer what it was, he learned that it had been taken out of a Buick and was intended for experimental use in a powerboat. He was staggered to learn that the engine had actually ceased production after only three years, when the American motoring public had turned its back on the 'compact' cars of the early 1960s. Measurements showed that it was just the right size to fit into the engine bays of both the P5 and the P6, and Martin-Hurst says now that he knew

The ex-General Motors V8 engine in P5B form.

right away he just had to have that engine for Rover. By 1964 it was being examined in Solihull; the Rover Company gained a licence to manufacture it in January 1965, and it went into production at Solihull as soon as was humanly possible after that.

The General Motors '215' (it displaced 215 cubic inches) had first appeared in autumn 1960 in the 1961 season 'compact' cars – the Buick Special, Pontiac Tempest and Oldsmobile F-85 Cutlass. In Buick and Pontiac form, it breathed through a twin-choke Rochester carburettor to give 155bhp at 4,600rpm and 220lb/ft of torque at 2,400rpm, while the Oldsmobile variety had different pistons and cylinder heads and a higher power output. All varieties were die-cast from a strong but lightweight aluminium alloy, and all had hydraulic self-adjusting tappets to promote quiet running.

Rover retained the engine's basic dimensions and layout,

The very first publicity shots were of YAC 636, a pre-production vehicle. Production Mk Is for the home market had no badging on the front wing; the triangular grille badge on this car is also reversed, with a black ship's sail on a red background. The louvres over the drop-glasses disappeared in 1961 when Mk IA models arrived, but the two-tone colour schemes remained available until the demise of the Mk IIs.

but made a number of other modifications. Instead of die-casting the blocks with the cylinder liners held in place, they went for sand-casting with press-fit liners. Breathing was improved to give a slightly higher rev range, and a new inlet manifold was designed to take twin SU carburettors in place of the Rochester. A manual choke control replaced the typically American automatic choke, and the compression ratio was raised to 10.5:1 to give a maximum power output of 184bhp at 5,200rpm and a torque figure of 226lb/ft at 3,000rpm. Those who worked at Solihull have commented that the degree of change wrought by Rover engineers on the American design is too often understated; that is probably true, but it should also be said that Rover would never have got to grips with an American V8 so quickly if they had not imported Joe Turley, Buick's chief engine designer, along with the engine. Turley, who was almost due to retire from GM, was delighted to help in the further development of what was, after all, one of 'his' engines.

The V8 weighed-in at 200lb less than Rover's faithful IOE 'six', so it took out the weight as well as putting in the

power. Weight distribution changed as well, the new model being less nose-heavy than the superseded one, and consequently it handled rather better despite some complaints that the lighter front end removed all traces of feel from the power steering. Although the P5B (B for the Buick engine) was no sports car, and was limited to a 115mph top speed because of the gearing which went with its automatic transmission, it could comfortably out-accelerate even the relatively quick manual-transmission 3-litre, and its fuel consumption was actually better than the superseded model's (though, in fairness, overdrive 3-litres were still more economical on long runs). That the P5 'chassis' design accepted all these extra strains and stresses without protest is an indication of the soundness of its basic concept.

There were no major revisions to the P5B engine before the model went out of production in the summer of 1973. From the beginning, it had an alternator instead of the 3-litre's dynamo, and the power-steering pump, dynamo-driven on the older model, became belt-driven direct from the crankshaft pulley. The first V8s wore rocker shafts very quickly, and the shaft material was changed quite early on. An automatic choke was fitted in 1968 (Rover called it an Automatic Enrichment Device or AED for short), but its reputation was destroyed partly because supply difficulties forced the factory to fit a number of cars with manual choke

controls, and partly because the device itself was never as reliable as Solihull would have liked. By 1974 Rover were shamefacedly offering a conversion kit to manual choke, and probably a high proportion of automatic chokes were replaced by frustrated owners.

Three different transmission options were available on the Mk I 3-litre cars: four-speed manual, four-speed manual with overdrive, and automatic. The automatic and non-overdrive cars shared a 3.9:1 axle ratio, while 4.3:1 was specified with the overdrive. Manual gearboxes were identical to the contemporary P4 items, with synchromesh on the three upper ratios, and the overdrive was the P4's Laycock DeNormanville unit with electrical control and a kickdown switch beneath the accelerator pedal. The gear lever of these early 3-litres was the familiar 'pot-stirrer' type also inherited from the P4.

Although the Roverdrive automatic transmission of the 105R had been tried during P5 development, it was found to overheat when installed behind the 3-litre engine, and so the automatic 3-litre had a Borg-Warner type DG box, a

The chrome strip above the rear number-plate was echoed on P4s after 1958. This is a Mk IA, with underlined marque name on the boot lid and no '3 litre' badging. The chromed fuel filler lid persisted until 1963. Photographed by Alan Milstead.

Looking altogether more purposeful than the Mk I is this Mk II 3-litre Saloon. Most of the exterior cosmetic changes had been introduced on the Mk IA models, but Mk IIs rode an inch lower on their suspension than earlier cars.

The 3-litre Coupe first appeared in Mk II form for the 1963 season. Two-tone arrangements differed from those of Saloons.

three-speed unit which was also used in contemporary Jaguars. This remained on the 3-litre's option list until the introduction of the Mk III models in autumn 1965, the only modifications coming with the Mk IA models, which had an adjustable electrically-operated intermediate gear hold in place of the earlier cable-operated control. The new control also permitted selection of bottom gear when starting from rest; shortly after the 3-litre's introduction, the automatic models had been modified to give a 'second speed start', a refinement introduced to give a smoother takeoff by eliminating one of the upward changes.

The non-overdrive cars were discontinued with the arrival of the 1961 season Mk Is, but changes to the manual gearbox itself had to wait until the introduction of the Mk II models the following year. These cars and the Mk IIIs which followed had raised second and third gear ratios, which gave a closer-spaced set of ratios and improved acceleration. The overdrive kickdown facility was discontinued because its use at the higher speeds of which these cars were capable could have caused overspeeding of the engine and unpleasant transmission snatch. Perhaps most important from the driver's point of view, the close-ratio gearbox was operated by a short remote-control gear lever sited on the transmission tunnel, which gave more precise selection than the infamous 'pot-stirrer', and incorporated as an additional refinement a pushbutton detent protecting reverse.

From autumn 1965, all automatics (special-order Mk IIs excepted) used the Borg-Warner type 35 gearbox, an improved unit of greater torque capacity offering smoother changes. This transmission had actually been tested in the V8 development programme when that engine had proved

A Mk III 3-litre Saloon. Principal external differences from earlier cars were the thicker trim strip and larger grille badge, together with 'Mk III' badging.

The 3.5-litre Coupe remains the most sought-after variant of the P5. This early two-tone car belonged to Rover's press fleet. Badging remained unchanged until the end of production, despite the redesignation of cars as 3½-litre models in autumn 1968.

too much for the DG box (a type 8 had also proved unsatisfactory), and it was not until then that its potential advantages for the 3-litre had become apparent. It permitted use of the 134bhp engine, which the DG box had not; it could be dropped from the car for servicing independently of the engine and subframe, which the DG box could not; and with new internal ratios combined with a 3.54:1 axle it gave acceleration which required fewer engine revolutions for the same effect and was consequently both quieter and (marginally) more economical. On Mk III models it was accompanied by an oil cooler fitted ahead of the radiator, and Rover took care to provide a long filler tube which emerged under the bonnet so that it was no longer necessary to remove the carpets to check the fluid level. Mk III automatics also had a different selector quadrant, which read PRNDL instead of the PNDLR of the DG-transmission cars, the changed reverse position being one of the earliest effects on Rover of American safety legislation.

A rather special 3.5-litre Saloon built for Prime Minister Harold Wilson in 1967. The apparently standard exterior belies the wealth of special features fitted to the car.

The 3-litre's manual gearbox – which dated in essence from the 1934 Rovers – was unable to cope with the V8's torque, and Rover had no other suitable unit available. The 3.5-litre cars, therefore, went into production with the automatic transmission as standard, and as Rover's Sales Division were convinced that a manual gearbox was not necessary in the big luxury saloon market, the car was never offered with anything other than the type 35 transmission. The 3-litre automatics had had their transmission selector on the steering column, but from the beginning of V8 production the selector was located on the centre console. For the first year of production, the 3.5-litres had an L-D1-D2 selector, but with the series B models for 1969 came both higher change-up speed settings and a 1-2-D selector range which gave a greater degree of manual override control but no longer permitted the smooth (and fuel-saving) second-speed start. There were no further transmission changes before P5B production was terminated.

The constant process of detail improvement which marked the P5's career was visible also in the braking and steering revisions introduced over the years. The first cars had a servo-assisted all-drum braking system generally similar to that of the P4 90 and 105, but from autumn 1959 Girling disc brakes were fitted to the front wheels. This was in response to market pressure rather than because the drum brakes were in any way inadequate, although it is probably true to say that some changes would have been necessary to cope with the increased speed of the Mk II models if the disc brakes had not already been specified. Later Mk Is and all Mk IAs had a vacuum reservoir tank for the servo, but Mk IIs and Mk IIIs did not. There were no more changes of note until the V8-engined models had a Lockheed servo instead of the original Girling type, together with harder disc pads to cope with the higher performance; the vacuum reservoir tank returned with this installation. From the beginning, the handbrake was a pull-out lever by the driver's outboard hand under the facia and, despite minor revisions to the linkage over the years, it was never one of the car's better points. As for steering, the Burman recirculating ball unit was supplemented from autumn 1959

Facia of a Mk I Automatic. The T-handle beside the cigar lighter was a highly inaccessible intermediate gear hold. Later models would differ considerably from the first production cars, even though the general layout of instruments and controls did not alter.

by an optional Hydrasteer variable-ratio power-assisted system, the first powered system on a production Rover. This was standard on all Coupes, and was then standardized on Mk IIC and later Saloons as well. The only significant change was in the pump drive already discussed, which came with the V8-engined models.

The P5's power-assisted steering has often been criticized for being too light, and for transmitting too little feel of the road to the driver. Certainly, the Hydrasteer system was primitive by later standards, but in the hands of a sensitive driver it gave no cause for worry. By contrast, the non-assisted steering of the first cars was considered too heavy, particularly at parking speeds, and Mk II Saloons were given a higher-geared steering box for the 1964 season, to become Mk IIB models (the 'B' suffix denoted the steering change; as all Coupes had PAS, they remained unchanged and retained the Mk IIA designation). At the same time, the hydraulic damper employed with manual steering was changed for a friction-type damper, which was perhaps cheaper but was neither adjustable nor serviceable.

Throughout the P5's life, suspension was by semi-elliptic variable-rate leaf springs at the rear, with laminated torsion bars for the independently-sprung front wheels. From the Mk II onwards, the ride height was reduced by an inch to give better handling properties. Certain export markets were supplied with cars which had heavy-duty rear springs (Rover called them 'high suspension' springs), and an 'H' stamped on the commission number plate identified these cars. All the cars were delivered with crossply tyres, normally of 6.70 section, although an option discontinued when the Mk IAs arrived was 7.10-section tyres. On the electrical side, a positive-earth system was used until the demise of the Mk IIs, when negative-earth electrics were introduced as part of a policy to permit the use of standard transistorized electrical components across the range.

There were two special export-only variants of the P5,

The interior of Mk I Saloons dated very quickly. This is one of the very first, with the original transverse pleating on the seats.

which were the first Rovers (simple LHD conversions apart) built exclusively for the export market. In both cases, smaller engines were fitted to circumvent penal tax jumps in the territories to which the cars were exported. Thus, from about spring 1962, France and Nigeria were offered a P5 model fitted with the 2,625cc 'Weslake head' engine of the P4 110 – the very model which had earlier been under consideration as an economy model for the home market. The 2.6-litre, as it was called, was identical in every way except for its engine and badging to the contemporary 3-litre Saloon; it first appeared in Mk IA guise and it ceased production as a Mk II in 1966. Sales were never high, despite the production of both LHD and RHD versions,

and of course acceleration and maximum speed were closer to those of Mk I 3-litres. Throughout its life, the 2.6-litre retained the P4-type wide-ratio gearbox of the Mk I/IA cars, which was better suited to its torque characteristics but, of course, detracted from all-out acceleration; there was never an automatic option. Even rarer – and slower – was the 2.4-litre model sold in Austria. No doubt the short-stroke IOE 'six' of 2,445cc had been developed with something else in mind, as it is inconceivable that it should have been built solely for a limited overseas market in one model. The story goes, however, that Rover's Austrian importers thought they could sell a 2.4-litre P5 in sensible quantities, and more or less badgered Solihull into making one. However, sales were very poor indeed, and the model was available for only a short time (roughly spring to summer 1962), while the engine was never used in another production Rover. Like the 2.6-litre, the car used the wide-ratio gearbox and was offered only with manual transmission; otherwise, it was identical to the contemporary 3-litre Saloons.

Bodies

The P5 body was styled by David Bache, working under Maurice Wilks' guidance. As usual, Wilks started with a pre-existing body shape – in this case that of the Farina fixed-head coupe on the P4 90 chassis – and adapted it. As Bache was a trained stylist, the finished product perhaps reflected as many of his ideas as of Wilks', but he has commented that it was not easy in those days to get his own way! The original design was for a four-light saloon, but once its basic shape had been established, Wilks asked his body team (the mid-1950s saw the creation of a Styling Department at Solihull for the first time) to draw up what was variously called a 'Sports Saloon', a 'Hard Top', or a '3-litre S' variant. Several designs were proposed, but the one eventually chosen for production simply added a lower roof and more steeply raked front and rear screens to the same lower body hull. As originally conceived, it had frameless side windows like the contemporary Mercedes-Benz coupes, but problems with these, plus the huge cost of tooling up for production, meant that only the Saloon version was approved for 1958 introduction; the 'Sports Saloon' body style was shelved and would not be made available until 1962.

In designing the P5's body, Rover tried to avoid the pitfalls of the P4 design. Thus the petrol tank was placed between the boot and the rear seat so that the boot floor was level and unobstructed; the spare wheel again lived in a tray beneath the boot floor, but this time the tray wound down to permit access; and the rear wing panels were bolted rather than welded to the main body structure, thus ensuring cheaper and easier accident repairs.

The production Saloon body relied for its effect on simple styling set off by subtly positioned trim lines. This was the classic Bache approach. Where the Farina body had hinted

It is difficult to see from this publicity shot of a Mk II Coupe interior how restricted was the rear leg room. Door trims, seats and gearbox tunnel carpeting have all changed from the Mk I/IA cars, and their general pattern was echoed on Saloon models, although this type of wood trim on the doors was a Coupe peculiarity.

at separate wings in its rear body side pressings, Bache's slab-sided P5 was relieved only by a slim chromed strip which terminated in a neat downturn over the front wheelarch. Badging was almost entirely absent, with only the 'Rover' name on the boot lid and a discreet 'Rover 3-litre' badge on the top bar of the wide radiator grille, which echoed the Farina design. There were no quarter-lights, but perspex louvres over the side windows, recalling the Rovers of the 1930s, were designed to give draught-free ventilation; as it turned out, they also created wind roar at speed and distorted vision! New hubcaps with a stylized Rover emblem recessed into the centre differed from the P4 pattern, and the body was longer, lower and wider than the P4, although there was a deliberate overall similarity, particularly in the car's frontal aspect.

seat or two individual seats could be had at the front. Deep pile carpets were fitted, but the headlining was plastic, like that introduced shortly before on P4 models. Although the passenger compartment really was longer than the P4's, an illusion of even greater space was created by setting the facia panel well forward; the glove boxes were shallower, but a parcel shelf running across the front at knee height compensated for the loss. Padded rolls all round indicated the first stirrings of Rover's interest in passive safety features, and the new pod-style instrument panel carried another 'first' in a Rover – a key-activated starter switch.

The original interior design had trim-coloured padding around the window frames, but this was changed in autumn 1960 when the wooden door cappings were extended all round the windows in the P4 manner. The transverse seat pleating was replaced by pleating running from front to back, and there were also changes to the headlining, the interior mirror, the air vents in the facia and the rear

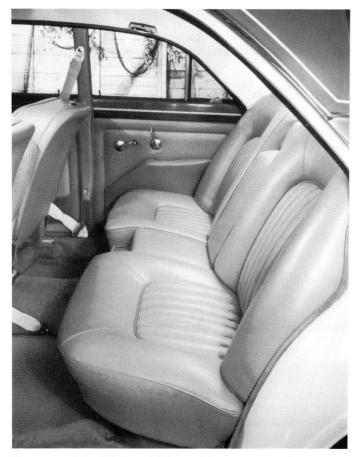

The seats of the Mk III and P5B models were eventually based on those designed for the 2000, although a more distinctive design had been tried experimentally.

The Mk I bodies had an attractive interior design, in which charcoal grey panels and instrument surround set off the main colour. The dashboard and door cappings were polished wood, while the seats had padded edge rolls with pleating running across the centre panels. Either a bench

It was possible to specify head restraints for the front seats of Mk IIIs and P5Bs, complete with a rear passenger's reading light.

courtesy lights, while automatic models had a new red 'handbrake on' warning light. The 1961 models all had stainless steel exterior trim in place of chrome-plated brass, and there was a small change to the fillet over the front wheelarch.

The P5 had always been intended to appeal to the chauffeur-drive market, and for the 1961 season the Radford coachbuilding concern introduced a detachable limousine division similar to that which they also marketed for the contemporary Rolls-Royce and Bentley models. This was a rather expensive extra, however, and probably no more than half a dozen were made before it was withdrawn in 1967; none are known to survive, although a single example of a similar division of unknown make survives on a 1969 model 3.5-litre Saloon.

Although there were important mechanical changes over the next four seasons, the alterations to body and interior were almost wholly cosmetic. The two-tone interior which had appeared so chic in the late 'fifties had dated quickly, and the grey contrast panels were deleted with the arrival of the Mk II models for the 1963 season. At the same time, there were new front armrests and the steering column/instrument panel assembly changed to black. Neater stainless steel trim appeared on the interior woodwork, and the window winder handles gained black plastic grips.

Fully-adjustable individual front seats had arrived as an option shortly after the autumn 1961 introduction of Mk IA models, and the repositioned gear lever on manual-transmission Mk II models meant that these cars had to have individual front seats of one sort or the other; on the automatics, the bench seat in fact became less common as time went on.

From the inside, Mk IIs were also distinguished from Mk IAs by clearer faces to the instruments, spade-shaped switches and a larger amber handbrake warning light (the red light had been standardized for both manual and automatic transmission on Mk IA cars), while Mk IIC models could be spotted by the revised switchgear occasioned by the introduction of twin-speed windscreen wipers, and by a pointer instead of a ring on the automatic transmission selector panel. Safety belts, which were first offered on Mk IAs, were not standardized until much later, although they were almost invariably fitted to the front seats of Mk II cars.

Colours and trim changed for Mk II production, but then remained constant until autumn 1966, and although Mk IAs could be distinguished from Mk Is by their larger stainless steel wheel trims, the presence of front quarter-lights and the absence of louvres over the side windows, Mk IIs were less easy to tell from Mk IAs. The keen-eyed would have

The Pressed Steel estate car conversion suffered from body rigidity problems and would have cost nearly twice as much as the standard Saloon if it had gone into production.

noticed a new grille badge and altered badging on the boot lid, while later Mk IIs could be identified by the painted fuel filler cap which replaced the chrome type during Mk IIB production in 1963. A number of the later cars were also fitted with Webasto's fabric sunroof, which became an approved extra for 1964.

The launch of the Mk III 3-litres was almost certainly brought forward as a sales ploy to revive interest in the car before the introduction of the V8-engined model, as the Mk II models remained available alongside them for a year (at a slightly lower cost), doubtless in an attempt to use up stocks of old parts. Changes to the outside of the Mk IIIs were restricted to new badging on the grille and boot lid, with 'Mk III' badges adorning the latter and the front wings. A thicker side trim strip was added, without the neat downturn over the front wheelarch, and it terminated in three symbolic pips on the rear wings. In addition, a new circular chromed petrol filler cap was fitted. Although two-tone Saloons were available during the 1966 season, the new style did not lend itself very well to this treatment, and

most cars were ordered in a single colour. When the colour options were revised for 1967, single colours were standardized on Saloons.

Just as the new grille badge was P6-derived (probably to create some kind of family unity between the two widely different ranges), so the new seats were a larger version of the lightweight P6 design. Their heavily padded edges gave much improved support, and adjustable front headrests with built-in reading lamps for rear passengers were offered as an optional extra. Saloon models could be supplied with either a rear seat split into two individual units, P6-fashion, or a traditional bench seat; but bench front seats were no longer available, and all individual front seats were now fully-adjustable. Rear headrests could also be specified for Saloons. There was a rear heater, with a fan operated from a switch panel on the transmission tunnel, and a new rear parcel shelf in the interior colour contained provision for an additional radio speaker, which could be controlled from a switch adjacent to the rear heater fan control. A steel reinforcing edge reappeared on the front parcel shelf, having been absent throughout Mk II production, and a 'modesty skirt' now shrouded the handbrake warning light. At the front, the tool tray was moved to the centre and given a veneer lid so that it doubled as a picnic tray; rear seat passengers had their own foldaway picnic tray concealed behind the armrest, as well as a trinket box between the seats on four-seater Saloon models. Detail revisions included the repositioning of the clock to the passenger's side corner fillet of the facia, where it now had a black bezel, and the loss of both map pockets and ashtrays from the front seat backs, the latter being recessed into the armrests on Saloon models. In addition, maximum gear speeds were marked on the speedometer in automatic Saloons.

If the Mk III 3-litres had represented a sort of 'halfway-house' between the Mk IIs and the 3.5-litre models, there was no mistaking the P5Bs when they were introduced in 1968. Instant recognition points were the fog lights sunk into the front wings below the headlamps, the chromed Rostyle wheels and the rubber-faced overriders. Less immediately obvious were a new gilded metal grille badge, the absence of the starting-handle support from the front number-plate box, and wider spacing of the Rover name on the boot lid. The side trim lost its three pips, and now contained repeater flashers on front and rear wings, while

there was an additional strip on the body sill, which was painted matt black in an attempt to slim down the side elevation; '3.5-litre' plate badges on front wings and boot lid, and a twin-barrelled exhaust tailpipe completed the transformation. There were to be no more external changes to the cars, although Sundym tinted glass became an option in 1969 and a Triplex Hotline heated rear window with yellow elements replaced the laminated type with concealed elements in 1971.

The V8-engined cars retained the Mk III 3-litre's interior, but with some small changes. A new console was constructed on the gearbox hump and carried the gear selector lever, an ashtray (displacing the plastic ones under the parcel shelf), and the cigar lighter and switch for the fog lights. The switch for the heated rear window was installed alongside when, as was almost invariably the case, that option was fitted to the car. There was additionally a small tray for trinkets ahead of the selector lever. Carpet colours were now limited to grey or beige, depending on seat colours. Next to the choke control was a T-handle for the petrol reserve control, which was now a mechanical component as there was a single fuel pump in place of the twin pumps of the 3-litre. The only other notable change was the loss of the oil level indicator switch which had been

This 3-litre drophead by FLM Panelcraft was made for a private customer and cost about £700, or around half the price of the car when new. Huge reinforcing irons were fitted beneath the trim strip on the body sills.

found on every other Rover (P4 80 and P6 models excepted) built under the Wilks regime.

Subsequent changes were all minor. A larger rear-view mirror was specified from March 1968, and from that autumn the gear lever knob had a cutaway centre, while the front ashtray gained a plain instead of a ribbed lid. Thinner front seat squabs also gave additional legroom in the rear. When the automatic choke was fitted (December 1968 on Coupes, February 1969 on Saloons), the choke control and warning light were both deleted. In January 1971, a thiefproof ignition lock was fitted and the keylock moved to a steering column position; at the same time, inertia-reel front seat belts were standardized, a modification to the B/C posts made in October 1969 having first permitted their fitting. An incidental change was that the P5Bs were renamed 3½-litres from autumn 1968 in an attempt to avoid confusion with the then new P6B 3500. Badging, however, was never altered.

Coupe bodies were introduced with the Mk II models for 1963, and in general they followed the same development as their Saloon counterparts; like these, they were built by the Pressed Steel Company at Swindon. They were readily recognizable by their lower roofline and raked front and rear screens; there was also a decorative stainless-steel plate on the rear quarter-pillars and a 'Coupe' badge on the boot lid. Only fully-adjustable individual front seats were available, while the rear seats were lower and set further forward than in Saloons in order to compensate for a loss of rear headroom. Right from the beginning of Coupe production the rear seats were fitted out as two individual units, and their central panel contained a 'smoker's companion' consisting of a cigar lighter and ashtray. The wooden door cappings were deeper than those of Saloon models and did not continue around the window frames, which on Coupes were of stainless steel. Sill buttons for the door locks were provided, and all Coupes had the rear parcel shelf in the interior trim colour. The only other differences were in instrumentation; a rev-counter replaced the Saloon's combined instruments dial, and the three displaced gauges were matched by an oil pressure gauge and mounted in twin binnacles under the main instrument pod. Two-tone Coupes were available until the end of P5B production and differed from two-tone Saloons by having the roof in one colour while the whole lower hull was in the second.

Not surprisingly, the P5's monocoque construction deterred the private coachbuilders from offering alternative body styles. Nevertheless, a few special-bodied cars were built. The earliest of these was an estate variant, converted from a 1959 Mk I Saloon by Pressed Steel, allegedly with the aim of demonstrating to the Rover Company that the 3-litre could rival the contemporary Humber estate cars. The car was evaluated at Solihull and the single prototype (some say that two were made) returned to Pressed Steel. The Rover Company themselves next commissioned a two-door drop-head prototype from the Parisian coachbuilder Chapron. The conversion was carried out in 1961 on an earlier Mk I Saloon, but it was evaluated in France by the Company's representatives and appears never to have come back to the UK. It is believed to have gone to a buyer in Switzerland, and so may well have inspired the Zurich coachbuilder Graber to construct a two-door convertible out of a left-hand-drive Saloon, which he then exhibited at the 1963 Geneva Motor Show. Several Solihull employees recall seeing a Farina-bodied 3-litre convertible, basically similar to the Farina P4 drophead, although their sightings lack documentary or photographic confirmation, and three more unconfirmed drophead 3-litres are said to have been built in the early 1960s by a firm in Feltham, Middlesex. The last known drophead 3-litre was built in 1964 for a private customer by FLM Panelcraft, of London, whose two-door conversion featured a four-light hood, unlike the other known cars, which were two-light designs. This latter car, which was also evaluated at Solihull, was last heard of in the West Country in the late 1970s. As for the others, all have disappeared except for the Graber drophead, which still survives in Switzerland.

CHAPTER 6

A Rover for the new generation

The P6 image-changer, 1963 – 1977

P6 2000 (1963-1973), 2000TC and Automatic (1966-1973), 2200SC, TC and Automatic (1973-1976); P6B 3500 (1968-1976) and 3500S (1971-1976); North American P6B 3500S (1969-1971)

Rover changed a lot in the 1950s. For a start, the prosperity brought by the Land-Rover meant that the Company could afford to be more ambitious and adventurous, and Maurice Wilk's engagement of David Bache had an outward sign of Rover's awareness that there were valid new ideas coming from a younger generation of engineers which could and should go into the Company's products. Solihull itself already had two brilliant young engineers on its staff in the shape of Peter Wilks and Spen King, and even before Maurice Wilks ceded his position as Chief Engineer to Robert Boyle in 1956, it had been decided that the 'younger generation' should be given its head. With Spencer and Maurice Wilks still in overall control, at least any radical new ideas would be very carefully scrutinized!

It would be wrong, however, to see in this a sudden change of heart in Rover's management. The fact was that the market was changing in the mid-1950s, and if Rover were to survive they had to respond to these changes. The British car market was becoming much less parochial and consequently more receptive to engineering innovation. Just as British cars had to compete with foreign (mostly European) products abroad, so they were now having to fight an increasing number of these cars on their home ground. The new cars were opening up new market sectors, but at the same time restricting old ones; the up-and-coming

executive no longer wanted a pale imitation of his boss' Rover 90, as Solihull found when they tried to sell the P4 60. He wanted a smart, rapid and practical car which reflected his own smartness, alertness and practicality. Yet he did not want to lose touch altogether with the wood-and-leather of the boardroom and his boss' car. So the P6 was conceived with two priorities in mind which were wholly new to Rover – the export market and the 'young executive' sector. At the same time, it had to be recognizably a Rover. That Solihull succeeded so well in all these design aims is demonstrated by the ambivalent reactions which the car has always provoked among Rover enthusiasts – many complain that it did not have enough of the Rover tradition in it, while others claim that it completely outshone any of its predecessors! Rover laughed all the way to the bank.

The P6 really materialized out of a series of 'ideas sessions' held in Robert Boyle's office. The agenda was rather loosely defined as discussions on a replacement model for the P4, and all kinds of weird and wonderful schemes – flat-four engines, rear engines, hydropneumatic suspension, front-wheel drive and so on – were proposed before some measure of agreement was reached in October 1957. Preliminary mockup and layout work was completed by the end of that year, and a firm specification was issued on New Year's Day 1958.

The specification of a lightweight saloon with a 103in wheelbase, built on a base-unit structure, was inherited from the original P5 proposals of 1953, when that car had been

P6/1, the first 2000 running prototype, is seen here on test during March 1959. It has the original shark nose and pillarless cabin design. The woollen tufts attached to the body were used to study air flow.

projected as a smaller car than the P4. The P6 was to be a four-seater with an engine of between 1,800cc and 2,000cc, capable of 100mph and giving better fuel economy than the P4 without loss of the traditional Rover qualities of durability, reliability and ride comfort. Considering that the P4 105S had only just become the first production Rover to attain 100mph, and that from 2.6 litres, this was a pretty tall order. The programme scheduled the launch of the new car for October 1961, which made that order even taller!

As things were to turn out, the P6 was granted an extra two years' development time. Rover realized that in order to build it they needed a new factory, space for which was readily available on the Solihull site. Building permission was not forthcoming from the Government of the day, however, whose employment policy was to create new jobs in depressed areas, not to attract more labour to the already populous West Midlands. Eventually, a bargain was struck in the autumn of 1960: Rover could build a new assembly block at Solihull provided they also built a new factory at Pengam, near Cardiff, for component manufacture. There

was now no chance that the P6 would be in production on schedule, and it was to be October 1963 before it actually appeared as the new Rover 2000 in the showrooms. Sadly, the P6 was the last Rover with which Maurice Wilks would be associated; he died a few weeks before it was revealed to the public.

Base and mechanical units
The base-unit structure of the P6 was hardly revolutionary, as some writers have suggested: Citroën relied on it for the DS models introduced in 1954, one of which was purchased by Rover in 1958 for examination. Nevertheless, it was an unusual method of construction, and for a company with an image as conservative as Rover's it represented a radically new departure. The P6 base-unit was in effect a steel skeleton which formed both the body-frame and the 'chassis'. All mechanical components were attached to it, and the P6 'skeleton' could be driven as a complete unit; indeed, all completed base-units were road-tested in this condition before the body panels were bolted into place.

Before letting the P6 prototypes loose on the roads, Rover disguised them with 'Talago' badges, and even set up a Talago Motor Company so that the name on the tax disc would not give the game away! The name came from the initials of T.L. Gawronski, who was P6 Project Engineer. Photograph by Alan Milstead; badge from the Geoff Kent Collection.

Although the base-unit was largely Robert Boyle's baby, chassis engineering was contributed by Gordon Bashford, who centred his whole concept of the car's ride and handling on the use of radial-ply tyres, which had never before been seen on a Rover. At the rear, he specified a sliding-joint De Dion set up with location by Watts linkages and fixed-length drive shafts, which gave most of the advantages of independent rear suspension without its complexity; it also pleased Spen King and Peter Wilks, who favoured such a layout after their experiences with the Rover Special racing car (see Chapter 7). Braking was by power-assisted discs on all four wheels, inboard at the rear to reduce unsprung weight, and there was Adamant hour-glass worm-and-roller steering. The front suspension was an odd design, with horizontal coil springs transferring the stresses to the front bulkhead; partly, it was conceived in order to leave a very

wide engine bay, as a gas turbine-powered P6 was under consideration for eventual production and its power unit was rather bulky. In the event, only a single prototype (T4) was built, but the wide engine bay was to prove a boon later when larger-engined P6s were developed.

The engine of the Rover 2000 was a completely new overhead-camshaft four-cylinder unit of 'square' dimensions, which displaced 1,978cc and put out 90bhp when installed. To keep height down in order to get the engine under the car's low bonnet, a Heron-head 'bowl-in-piston' design was used. The Company's Sales Division, in fact, had been strongly opposed to the idea of a four-cylinder engine from the beginning as they had never had much success with the four-cylinder P4 60, and Maurice Wilks had had severe reservations at first about using an overhead camshaft, which he thought would be noisy. To be honest, the 2000's engine was never anywhere near as quiet and refined as the IOE

The gas turbine T4 was made from the 10th prototype P6 (P6/10). When it appeared, in 1961, the public could not have known that it embodied most of the shape of the forthcoming new Rover. Although small changes have been made over the years, the extended shovel-nose remains substantially as it was originally built.

The P6's base-unit. The idea had been seen before in the Citroen DS 19, but Rover had been toying with this method of construction in 1953, over a year before the Citroen was launched.

units of the P3s, P4s and P5s, but for a large four-cylinder it was certainly above contemporary standards. Although there had been all kinds of problems during development, the free-revving, lusty little engine which went into production was able to haul the car beyond its 100mph design target when required. Like all Rover engines built under the Wilks regime, it soon acquired a reputation for longevity and reliability – and this time for fuel economy, too. Its frugal petrol consumption enabled Rover to avoid the additional cost of an overdrive (although one was later tried experimentally), and the 2000 had nothing more complicated than a four-speed all-synchromesh gearbox, designed specifically for it and mated to a fairly high final drive of 3.54:1. The well-chosen ratios of the gearbox meant that acceleration was always available when required, and despite a rather notchy change mechanism, the remote-control gear lever actively encouraged the driver to make use of his gearbox.

Right from the design stage, Solihull's engineers had tried to build safety into the 2000, an aim which was almost unique in the late 1950s. Everything possible was done to make the car both actively safe (to avoid accidents) and passively safe (to protect the occupants if they were involved in one), and the Rover 2000 was awarded the AA's Gold Medal in 1965 for its outstanding contribution to safer motoring. Safe did not mean boring, however, and the car's superb roadholding, excellent gearbox and first-class brakes and steering made it a driver's car quite unlike previous Rovers, with an appeal way beyond the traditional Rover market. Triumph's rival 2000, launched shortly afterwards, was positively agricultural in comparison. Contemporary road-testers went into ecstasies when they first got their hands on a P6, but several of them pointed out that the car's chassis design was too good for its engine and that the P6 literally cried out for more power.

To be fair to Rover, this became abundantly apparent to

The unorthodox front suspension, so designed to leave an engine bay wide enough for the gas turbine engine Rover hoped to offer eventually.

them during the car's development. A gas turbine option might have fitted the bill, but it was still a long way off, and in any case it looked like being expensive. What was wanted was a more powerful petrol engine, and quickly. The IOE engines were too tall and too heavy, so in 1962 Jack Swaine's department started work on a six-cylinder variant of the 2000 engine, which used the same bore and stroke to arrive at a swept volume of 2,967cc. This certainly put in the power, but it was also half as long again as the 'four', and installation involved lengthening the front end of the car, which entailed major alterations to the base-unit as well as new panelling. The car was going to be so different with

this engine that it was given its own designation of P7.

Although Solihull seriously considered putting it into production, the P7 promised to be expensive in terms of new body tooling, so Robert Boyle suggested in 1964 that it might be worthwhile looking into a 2½-litre five-cylinder engine based on the 'four', which would have the advantage that it could just be squeezed into the existing P6 engine bay. Five-cylinder car engines were unheard-of in those days of course, although five-cylinder diesel engines for commercial vehicles had existed for some time, and Rover's engine designers set to with enthusiasm. They were working on problems of in-car balance for the 2,472cc units which were

The De Dion rear end gave exceptionally good roadholding, and ride comfort better than that of any Rover before or since. Changing pads on the inboard disc brakes was not to be the easiest of jobs, however.

running at the end of 1964, when both the five-cylinder engine and the P7 project were cancelled in favour of the 3½-litre V8 which Managing Director William Martin-Hurst had bought from General Motors in America.

Curiously, the P7 project was directly responsible for the naming of the P6 as the Rover 2000. Solihull's Sales Division had wanted to call it the 2-litre, but Martin-Hurst had pointed out to them that the P7 would then logically have to be called a 3-litre, and Rover already had a model by that name. So the name 2000 was chosen, much against the Sales Division's better judgment, with the name of 3000 in reserve for the P7 car.

Meanwhile, running more or less in parallel with the P7 and the five-cylinder projects had been a development programme on the four-cylinder engine. Jack Swaine's team found that by substituting bigger twin SU carburettors for the 2000's single SU, increasing the compression ratio to 10:1 and splitting the inlet manifold from the cylinder head (just as had been done for the IOE engines in 1962), they could get 124bhp out of the 1,978cc engine. A revised camshaft profile ensured that plenty of this new-found power was available at high rpm. As the five-cylinder 2½-litre was only putting out 125bhp or thereabouts, it was not surprising that the twin-carburettor engine was seized

In TC form, with twin SUs, the 1,978cc OHC engine gave 124bhp. Twin Weber 40 DCOEs had been tried during development, but they made the engine too intractable. In the search for more power, Rover had even fitted one development car with a Shorrocks supercharger, while Derrington offered a bolt-on twin-choke Weber conversion for the SC, which allegedly gave that car better performance than the production TC.

upon with enthusiasm by Rover's management and put into production as soon as it had proved itself (and gathered some advance publicity) in the works rally cars during 1964-65. Original plans were to introduce a plain 2000TC which would simply add the new engine to the base-model's specification, and a more sporting 2000S which would have the TC engine, wire wheels and various minor cosmetic alterations. In the end, the 2000S never got as far as the showrooms, although 15 cars were built, and its sporting

extras became options on the 2000TC.

The 2000TC was designed with the export market very firmly in view, so it was first seen in the European shop-window of the Geneva Motor Show in spring 1966. Home market models, which lacked some of the cosmetic innovations found on export cars, appeared that autumn. They were enthusiastically received; the TC offered vastly improved performance, with a top speed approaching 110mph and acceleration which put it into the sports car

This prototype five-cylinder engine, photographed by Alan Milstead, is now preserved by BL Heritage. Weld seams on sump, cylinder head, rocker cover and air cleaner show that standard engines were 'cut and shut' to build the prototypes.

Before the crunch. The 3500 V8 engine installed in a P6 which is about to be subjected to the mandatory crash test at MIRA in 1970.

One that got away. A fuel-injected version of the V8 engine was planned for 1971 introduction, and the car (with manual transmission) would have been badged as a 3500EI, presumably standing for Electronic Injection, as the set of badges shows.

class. Without a doubt, it lost something in refinement as compared to the base model, and its fuel consumption was not as good, but it did provide an attractive alternative to the poorly-constructed European slingshots which were the only real performance saloons available at the time in the same price bracket. Most important of all to Rover was the American market, where the TC's reception by the motoring press was ecstatic; unfortunately, its relatively high purchase price seems to have deterred that nation's buyers, and the car ultimately failed to achieve what Rover had hoped for it there, despite heavy promotion of its safety features as well as its performance.

Introduced at the same time as the TC was the 2000

These two pictures show how the early production 2000s looked. Cars made between 1963 and 1966 had a single central reversing lamp, with reflectors incorporated in the tail-lamp clusters. Prior to 1968, the wheel covers had only a single decorative ring.

A longer nose was needed for the P7 six-cylinder cars. The first car, 17 EXK, was cobbled together, but by the time of the fourth prototype in 1964 (there were five altogether) Rover's stylists had come up with an attractive new front end.

Automatic. There were those at Solihull who thought it should never have been made, because it was far slower than the standard 2000, and the last thing the P6 needed was less performance. Nevertheless, Rover's Sales Division insisted that there was an 'old gentleman's' market for such a car, and this time they were proved right. Development began in about 1964, and the car was rushed through to production. It shared its Borg-Warner type 35 transmission with the Mk III 3-litre introduced in 1965, and used the same final drive as the standard 2000. As contemporary road tests noted, it lacked urge for acceleration because the torque band of the 2000 engine was really too narrow to suit an automatic transmission; it had to rev harder than the manual gearbox car to achieve the same speeds and so was noisier; and it used more petrol in return for less performance. That so many customers bought it is probably an indication of how

much the old sedate Rover image still overshadowed the radically different P6 in the mid-1960s!

Development of the base-model had, of course, never abated, and literally hundreds of minor improvements were introduced in the two-and-a-half years before the arrival of the TC and Automatic models. Among the most important were a new steering damper, which arrived in 1964, rear suspension changes in 1965, and a more powerful brake servo allied to new pad material in mid-1965. The cable-drive windscreen wipers were replaced by link-driven wipers, and there were also improvements to the cooling system.

The base model was redesignated 2000SC when the TC and Automatic models arrived, although it was never rebadged. While the very first TC models shared the positive-earth electrical system of the 2000, all three models

47 GYK was sold to Ted Eves of *Autocar,* and is now owned by a Rover enthusiast. Despite later claims that P7s were not as quick as the V8-engined P6Bs, the Experimental Department saw a genuine 140mph from this car – and the heavy nose even improved its handling!

changed to negative earth for the 1966 season to permit the use of standard transistorized electrical components. From about May 1966, Girling brakes replaced the original Dunlops; Girling had actually absorbed the Dunlop braking interests, but the new brakes also represented a distinct improvement, being both easier to service and less prone to the sticking pistons which in extreme cases could cause broken discs in the Dunlop installation. Nevertheless, early Girling-equipped cars had to be recalled when a brake pipe was found to chafe on the differential extension tube. Then, in the autumn of 1966, SC and Automatic models were given a new twin-silencer exhaust system. All three 2000 models gained a crossflow radiator in place of the vertical-flow type in 1968, and there was a repositioned carburettor air intake on the SC models, designed to avoid carburettor icing problems by picking up warm air from behind the radiator. The transmission oil cooler incorporated in the radiator on early TCs was now deleted, although it remained available as an option.

That 2000 developments were less numerous in the 1966-68 period is doubtless a reflection of the Company's preoccupation with work on the ex-Buick V8 engine. The story of how this 3½-litre power unit came to Rover has already been told (see Chapter 5), but it is interesting that when it first arrived at Solihull, Chief Engineer Peter Wilks failed to share his Managing Director's enthusiasm for it, pleading pressure of work from other projects. Not to be thwarted, William Martin-Hurst prevailed upon the Competitions Department, who had little to do because of a lull between rallies, to cut about a 2000 development car and bolt the Buick engine into it. He then took Spencer Wilks for a rapid motorway run in the car. Wilks senior was convinced at once, with the result that the V8 became a Rover engine in short order. Although the P5 was actually first into production with the new engine, most of the development work was carried out with P6 cars right from

The sporting image of the 2000TC was much enhanced by its optional wire wheels, which nevertheless remained rare and ceased to be available in late 1969. Without them, the TC could only be distinguished from the other 2000s by its badging.

the beginning.

Martin-Hurst had been quite right in his assessment that the V8 would fit into the P6 engine bay, but the adaptation was far from straightforward. A second development car was rebuilt around a Buick engine, with a minimum of panel alteration, but the cost penalty of production in this form would have been unacceptably high. In the end, Rover's engineers moved the front crossmember of the base-unit forwards, put the battery in the boot and canted the engine backwards slightly to get what they wanted – no increase in overall length, no undue front axle weight and no need for new bonnet or front wing panels. With detail alterations to the inner wings, and bonnet stiffeners modified to clear the repositioned crossmember, the V8 installation was complete.

Like the P7 engine before it, the V8 produced too much torque for the standard 2000 gearbox, so five of the six development cars were fitted with ZF five-speed gearboxes (the sixth had automatic transmission). Rover felt the ZF boxes were too unrefined, and after the 1967 Leyland takeover, they tried a Triumph 2000 gearbox in desperation. That was not the answer, either, and as there was no time to develop a new manual gearbox, the P6B (B for Buick again) went into production with a Borg-Warner type 35 automatic

transmission as the only available option. A stronger final drive casing was fitted to cope with the V8's torque and a higher 3.08:1 ratio aided fuel consumption and ensured a greater top speed than the four-cylinder cars; acceleration was no problem, even with the automatic gearbox! The V8-engined cars also had larger radiators, modified rear suspension mountings, increased spring rates and stronger dampers. Braking was improved by larger front discs and a bigger servo, while fatter tyres on wider offset wheels necessitated small changes in the front hubs in order to maintain the original track and turning circle.

The 3500, or Three Thousand Five as it was renamed at the last minute, was launched in April 1968 to an enthusiastic reception, although more than one commentator lamented the absence of a manual gearbox option. As usual, Rover were to be disappointed over export sales, but there were still high hopes of cracking the North American market, and for this purpose a special version of the P6B was introduced for the 1970 season. Not much needs to be said about the mechanical side of the 3500S, except that its exhaust emission-control equipment, Adwest Varamatic power-assisted steering and optional air conditioning all took engine power away from the back wheels, where it was needed most. It could still outrun a 2000TC, but only just, and of course its fuel consumption had suffered. Dual-circuit braking looked good on the specification, and was never found on a home market P6, but the North American 3500S was a sales disaster. Only just over 2,000 were built, and the last of these were shipped hurriedly back to continental Europe for sale through Rover's dealer network there when the model was withdrawn in 1971. The stock of engines fitted with exhaust emission control was used up in the 1971 season home market 3500 cars with air conditioning.

The home market 3500 continued without significant mechanical change until the Mk II models arrived in the autumn of 1970. For 2000 models, the change to Mk II was marked by the introduction of an alternator in place of the dynamo, and by carburettor changes which had been brought about in the wake of emission-control development work. Base-unit commonization was served by putting the battery into the boot, 3500-fashion. The power-assisted steering first seen on the North American 3500S now became an option on the 3500, and the air conditioning system could also be specified at extra cost, although in practice it rarely was. The 2000TC models were given a distributor rev-limiter early in the 1971 season, governing engine speed to a 6,500rpm maximum. It seems that some owners had ignored the tachometer redline, probably in an attempt to out-accelerate hard-driven 3500s!

Much more interesting, however, was the October 1971 introduction of the long-awaited manual-transmission V8 model, which confusingly inherited the 3500S designation. The new gearbox in this car was simply an uprated 2000 four-speeder, with a strengthened and finned case, a much greater oil capacity and an oil pump driven from the rear of the layshaft. The gears themselves were shot-peened, and there were tougher layshaft bearings. Although the new clutch was criticized for being on the heavy side, no-one criticized the effect of the new transmission. The 3500S could cover the 0-60mph dash in a fraction over 9 seconds, gave vigorous acceleration right across its speed range, and peaked at 120mph or more – yet it still returned 25mpg. It had particular appeal as a Police chase car, as it undercut the price of the similarly rapid Jaguars by a huge margin, and

First thoughts on a facelift for the V8-engined cars included this late 1965 design with very Vauxhall-like styling details....

offered cheaper running costs as well. For the family motorist or executive it offered all the refinements and advantages of the 3500 (although certain cosmetic items standard on that car were extra-cost options on the 3500S), while giving him the opportunity to let his hair down with a real road-burner of a car at weekends. Not surprisingly, it was a big sales success.

Several changes to existing models coincided with the launch of the 3500S. The old four-fuse electrical system was replaced by the 12 fuse system of the North American 3500S. Manual transmission cars now had the gear lever attached directly to a gearbox extension, and there were internal changes to the 2000's manual gearbox. The 2000 models also received a pre-engaged starter, while the V8s were fitted with HIF type carburettors. All engines were now numbered in a Mk II series (1971 season Mk II cars

....but this was what went into production. This Three Thousand Five sports the revised wheel trims introduced in 1968 for all models, although the very first V8 cars had trims with the single central ring and improved claw fixings.

having in all cases Mk I engines). Subsequently, the V8 models were given a new alternator and starter motor, while the 2000 models were treated to yet another variety of exhaust system, this time with three silencer boxes, in an attempt to cut down the resonance which had plagued the four-cylinder cars ever since their introduction.

If the 3500S took the P6 into the high-performance class where it had really belonged from the beginning the four-cylinder models were beginning to look decidedly slow by the early 1970s. If road-test figures are to be trusted, the changes over the years had actually impaired their performance by comparison with early models, and to some extent the Rover 2000 had assumed the mantle of the earlier P4s and P5s – a good, sensible car without much performance. The problem was compounded because the cheap end of the

executive market at which the 2000 had originally been pitched was demanding – and getting – more and more performance. Rover therefore started to look around for ways of giving the four-cylinder models more punch.

For a time, Solihull considered giving the P6 a new four-cylinder 2,205cc DOHC engine, which was also intended in the longer term for use in the cheaper versions of the P10. Early in 1971, the P10 became a joint Rover-Triumph project (see Chapter 7), and a six-cylinder Triumph engine was planned for the cheaper models. As the DOHC engine now had no long-term future its development was aborted. Designed by David Wall to be machined on existing P6 transfer line tooling, it had a projected power output of between 120 and 145bhp (although fuel-injected prototypes gave 170bhp) and would have been installed with

Export models often differed in detail from their home market equivalents, and this attractive beast is a Three Thousand Five to German specification. The Rostyle wheels, thin side trim strips and racing mirror were available in the UK, but the problem was finding a dealer who knew that!

a slant of 35 degrees to ensure underbonnet clearance. One prototype of the engine, which was the last all-new, all-Rover, power unit ever designed, is preserved by BL Heritage.

With the slant-four option gone, Rover turned to an over-bored 2000 unit, also of 2,205cc capacity, for the revamped 'small' P6. New carburettors anticipated European emission-control regulations, and effectively prevented the full performance potential from being realized, but the larger engine's wider torque band gave the autumn 1973 2200 models (SC, TC and SC Automatic) a flexibility and mid-range urge which had been absent from the smaller 'fours'; the Automatic particularly benefited. Unfortunately fuel consumption was worse on all versions, although this seemed to matter little in the days before the Yom Kippur War when the 2200 was being developed, and there was some compensation in the engine's greater refinement. There were also improved ignition suppression and engine warm-up on the TC, the latter achieved by a thermostatically-controlled engine air intake.

Parts standardization and the increase in engine torque meant that the 2200 models inherited the stronger differential design and rear suspension of the 3500 variants. Although 2200SC Automatics retained the 2000's Borg-

Warner type 35 gearbox, the 3500 models had a new type 65 gearbox; lighter than the type 35, it offered smoother changes and was said to be more durable. The same year, the 3500 and 3500S became the first cars in the world to be offered with Dunlop Denovo run-flat tyres as an extra-cost option, available only with PAS. Early examples of these tyres gained a reputation for rapid wear, however, and relatively few P6Bs were so equipped. Meanwhile, 1974 season V8 engines had new pistons to give a lower compression ratio suitable for four-star (97 octane) fuel, although the consequent power and acceleration losses were never acknowledged in Rover literature. To some extent, the power loss (around 7bhp overall) was offset on the automatics because they now had the bigger-bore exhaust system of the 'S', which restored about 6bhp and gave the two models identical power outputs. Mechanical specification of all models thereafter remained without significant change until P6 production ceased in 1976, the V8 models ceding to the new SD1 3500 in the summer of that year and the 2200s continuing until Christmas, when the P6 lines were finally closed down. The very last car – a left-hand-drive 2200TC – was inexplicably sold off, but BL Heritage were able to preserve the last of the V8-engined cars. The 2200 models remained catalogued until the summer of 1977,

Another export car – this time a North American 3500S. Note the air scoops, fatter front bumper, bolt-through wheel trims, Icelert sensor and additional lights. The thicker side trim strips were later standardized on Mk II cars, and the blacked-out horizontal surfaces of the grille were inspired by Zagato's TCZ prototype.

but thereafter were replaced by the SD1 2300 model.

Although the 3,528cc V8 was the largest engine offered in production cars, British Leyland did build two 4½-litre cars for racing (see Chapter 7), and eight 4500 models are said to have been assembled in Australia, using the 4,416cc long-stroke version of the V8 originally developed for the P8 saloon, but only put into production in Australia in 1973 for Leyland Australia's products. In standard form, as fitted to the Leyland P76 car, this engine developed 192bhp at 4,250rpm and 285lb/ft of torque at 2,500rpm (SAE gross figures), although some production versions were made in a higher state of tune. The Rover 4500s were allegedly capable of 130mph.

Body and interior
From beginning to end of its 13½-year production run, the P6 used basically the same bodyshell. In the early days of the car's conception, David Bache – designing this time in his own right – had reasoned that the base-unit construction with bolt-on panels would make subsequent facelifts via restyled panels both cheap and easy, but no such facelift ever came about, and an early plan for a two-door Sports model never progressed beyond the mock-up stage. The only styling changes introduced were cosmetic, which perhaps suggests as much as anything that Bache got the shape right first time and that there was never any need for new panel designs!

Before production commenced, however, Bache had a hard time 'getting it right'. His first thoughts for the P6 were strongly reminiscent of Virgil Exner's 1956 Chrysler Dart prototype (rather than of Citroen's DS, as is commonly supposed). At the time, Bache was keen on American styling, and his first quarter-scale clays featured tailfins as well as the sloping nose shared by the Dart and the DS. Maurice Wilks and Robert Boyle soon talked him out of the tailfins, but the sloping nose was still in evidence by the time of the first P6 prototype in February 1959. Spencer and Maurice Wilks were not happy, however, and the collective foot of management was put firmly down the following year. All subsequent prototypes (about six had already been built)

This Mk II 2000 displays a number of optional extras including front seat head restraints, overriders and the boot lid mounting for the spare wheel (covered by a decorative disc bearing the Rover emblem). The reversing lights had been incorporated in the lamp clusters since 1966, while the reflectors had moved from boot lid to wings in 1971. Badging apart, 2200 models would be visually identical.

had the familiar production nose design, which cost the car some 5mph in top speed through its inferior aerodynamics. Typically for the early 1960s, the new nose featured an American-inspired twin headlamp arrangement.

The P6 body could not have been more unlike its predecessors. Lower and less fussy-looking, it retained an air of dignity which gave it credible links with Rover's past, but the patrician image of the P4s and P5s had gone. Trim-strips were out, and badging was kept to a minimum in the best Rover tradition. Bache relied on simple styling with just a body swage-line to bring down the high waistline characteristic of all his Rover designs (both the P5 and the SD1 have it too). The whole design had a classical elegance and a timelessness which even transcended the arrival of curved side window glass in the early 1960s, a styling catalyst which gave designers greater freedom in the shapes of their

passenger cabins. In prototype form, the petrol tank was installed under the boot floor, but this overstressed the rear of the base-unit, and so the tank was resited above the back axle. William Martin-Hurst worried that the boot was now too small, so he persuaded Maurice Wilks to engineer a large recess into the boot floor (after the body tools had been made!) and to make available an optional external mounting for the spare wheel on the boot lid so that more space was freed for luggage.

Changes to the appearance of the standard home market 2000 were minimal before the introduction of Mk II models in 1970. A locking petrol cap was standardized during 1965 and a new front lower valance was fitted the following year, which gave better airflow to the radiator and allegedly increased the top speed by about 1mph. The 1966 season cars had twin reversing lamps incorporated in the tail-light

The quickest production P6 of all, a manual-transmission 3500S. Like all Mk II models, this car has the new bonnet panel and grille, new door handles, plate-type badges and side trim strips. Blacked-out sills and vinyl-covered rear quarter-panels were also Mk II features, but the vinyl roof was peculiar to the 3500S at first. The early 3500S cars had the bolt-through wheel trims seen in this picture.

clusters instead of the single central lamp of the first cars, and the reflectors displaced by this change were resited on the bottom corners of the boot lid. The 1969 models all had new hubcaps with improved claw fixings (the earlier ones tended to rotate and could even cut through tyre valves), which were identified by two black rings in the centre. During that season, a new through-flow ventilation system was introduced, with flap valves concealed within the rear quarter-pillars. The opening rear quarter-lights were now redundant and were replaced by fixed panes, but within a year the original system had been reinstated. All the four-cylinder Mk I cars had chromed 2000 badges on the boot lid and front wings, plus TC badges in both these places and on the bonnet when appropriate. Automatics were so identified by an additional badge on the boot lid and a few early cars also had this badge on the front wings. Some of the very last Mk I cars actually had the badging associated with Mk IIs, probably because stocks of the earlier badges ran out before the planned changeover.

Options, of course, were legion, although many of them remained rare because they were little publicized. One which was frequently seen was the Webasto fabric sunroof, which was an approved post-factory extra from the beginning; almost never seen, however, were the two types of sliding steel sunroof offered after autumn 1968 (by Coenan and Hollandia) and the glass roof panel, produced by Triplex in conjunction with Rover, and available from 1969 as a post-factory fitting by Roof Installations Ltd. It had a zip-in headlining, so that the car could be used as a normal closed saloon, or as a splendidly light and airy vehicle without the disadvantages of a convertible top.

It was possible to have as options on the home market 2000s many of the features which were standard on Export models. Thus, from 1966, a thin stainless steel trim strip could be added along the body swage-line, chromed Rostyle wheels were available and rubber-faced overriders of a pleasant squat design could be specified. The Icelert system, a temperature sensor fitted ahead of the grille which lit a dashboard light to warn of the possibility of ice on the roads, was also available. In practice, though, these options

The neat and impressive dashboard layout of a 1967 2000TC.

The P6's main fault was a lack of interior space, particularly in the rear. These are the box-pleated Ambla seats standard on the original 3500S; on other models, leather seat facings were standard until 1973, when nylon cloth took over.

This revised instrument panel was first seen on the North American 3500S, and was standardized on Mk II V8 and 2000TC models.

were rarely taken up by home market customers. Equally rare were the wire wheels available on TC models, and an alternative design of rubber-faced overrider which was introduced in 1965 but remained unpopular because it did not suit the P6 shape at all. North American customers could specify a second type of Rostyle wheel, a rather vulgar creation known as the MagStar, but this was never available in the UK. A heated rear window was a popular option from the beginning, as were front fog lights slung under the bumper, but Sundym tinted glass and Delaney Gallay air conditioning, both introduced in August 1969, were rarely seen on home market cars.

Body differences for the Three Thousand Five were kept to a minimum, but the cars were instantly recognizable by a heavy stainless steel 'eyebrow' at the leading edge of the bonnet and a deeper front valance to accommodate the larger radiator. In addition, the squat rubber-faced overriders were standard, and there were 3500 plate-type badges (engraved rather than printed like the Mk II variety) on wings, grille and boot lid, plus 'V8' badges on the bonnet and boot lid.

Sharp eyes might also have spotted a new lashing ring at the front of the base-unit and a thinner surround to the triangular grille badge than on the 2000.

The first indications of Rover's thinking about the forthcoming Mk II models were given by the North American 3500S cars when they appeared for the 1970 season. These had new bolt-through wheel trims of a sporty 'spoked' design, and side trim strips which were noticeably wider than the early optional or Export type; twin door mirrors were also fitted. The Icelert system was standard, and the cars were also distinguished by a number of features which would never be available for the home market. Thus, there were a fatter front bumper and three air intake scoops on the bonnet to aid engine bay cooling, while the horizontal surfaces of the grille were blacked-out (an idea derived from the 1965 Zagato coupe prototype). A painted coachline was also added above the side trim strip, and the cars had the special side lights and marker lights demanded by US Federal Regulations. These same regulations obliged Rover to incorporate crash-reinforcement bars inside the doors.

The prototype 2000 two-door drophead by FLM Panelcraft was commissioned by Rover in 1965. It is currently owned by the author. The roof panel of Triplex Sundym glass fitted to the 2000TC was designed to demonstrate how glass could be used in vehicle construction as an alternative to metal.

Although the 3500S Automatics were allegedly produced in both Mk I and Mk II forms, they were always curious hybrids, and in fact some of the Mk I cars sold off in Europe were updated by dealers with Mk II grilles.

All the Mk II P6s used the 3500 base-unit with its revised front crossmember and the battery box in the boot. Known in sales literature as 'New Look' models, they were distinguished by a black plastic radiator grille, the thick side trim strips of the 3500S Automatics, new hubcaps with a black centre panel, and a bonnet with two 'power bulges',

which in fact acted as stiffeners and replaced the cross-bracing found inside earlier bonnets. All Mk IIs had black or (less commonly) brown vinyl panels on the rear quarter-pillars, with a P5 Coupe-style Viking ship badge, and from autumn 1971 customers could specify as an option on the 3500 the matching vinyl roof covering which was standard on the new 3500S. In all cases, the body sills were painted to match the vinyl panels in an attempt to slim the car's side elevation. The TC models had rubber-faced overriders like the V8s, and the few 1971 season cars

The 2200SC, introduced in 1973 and featuring an over-bored version of the 2000 engine, brought a welcome improvement in torque, but a less pleasing increase in fuel consumption.

(mainly 3500s) fitted with air conditioning had a single air scoop on the bonnet, though later air conditioned cars dispensed with this. New door handles on the Mk IIs looked neater than the early type, and the rear reflectors were repositioned below the light clusters as part of a series of rear-end changes. The marque name moved from the centre of the boot lid to its bottom left-hand corner, while other changes were to the '2000' badge (which was now in aluminium with a black background) and to the position of the triangular grille badge (resited on the bonnet). The 'V8' and 'TC' badges moved from bonnet to grille, and the 3500 – the Three Thousand Five name chosen by William Martin-Hurst was now dropped – lost its 'eyebrow'. Further badging alterations accompanied the launch of the manual-transmission 3500S in autumn 1971; plate-type badges replaced the 2000's model badge, matching badges on all cars bore the 'Rover' name on the boot lid, and Borg-Warner-equipped 2000s lost their 'Automatic' badge.

The 3500S models inherited the bolt-through wheel trims of their North American namesakes (and supplies were also used up on certain other Export vehicles), but were fitted with the standard trims after autumn 1973. On this date, which coincided with the launch of the 2200 models, all cars were fitted with a driver's door mirror as standard to conform to new EEC Regulations. The heated rear window was now standard in all but certain Export markets, and Sundym glass was standardized on V8-engined models. All the P6 cars built from early 1976 were sprayed in the new paint plant built for the SD1 at Solihull, using SD1 colours and the new 'oven-bake' paint process. In order to facilitate this, body panels met their base-units earlier in the assembly process than had hitherto been the case. Sadly, the new paint process had teething troubles, and Rover were plagued with warranty claims on these last P6s (as on early SD1s) when the paint started to flake. A batch of 150 of the last 3500 models was built as a 'limited edition', and these cars were known in the trade as 'VIP' models. All were finished in Platinum, the silver metallic paint used on SD1s, but not otherwise available on the P6.

The story of the P6's interior development is no less

102

Zagato's Lancia-like styling exercise on a 2000S – the TCZ. Changes of registration number have fuelled unfounded rumours that more than one car was built. The TCZ has been restored by an enthusiast, and is seen here at a club rally in 1982, when it was photgraphed by Lesley Ann Taylor.

David Bache's two-door hatchback coupe based on a Three Thousand Five was built for Rover by Harold Radford in 1967. It has always been known at Rover as 'Gladys'. The nose recalls P7 designs, the bonnet bulges appeared on Mk II P6s, and the box-pleated seats are pure 3500S. Bache now owns this car, which allegedly cost £22,000 to build.

complicated than that of its exterior appearance. When it was launched in 1963, its leather-covered seats were of completely new design, light in weight and carefully padded for optimum body support, and the rear seat was designed strictly to seat two. Some contemporary road tests described these seats as the most comfortable available in any car, bar none. Weight and cost had also been saved by the use of Formica imitation wood on plastic strips for the door cappings and on the dashboard (although a batch of early cars did have real wood veneer trim). The dashboard itself was an entirely new design by David Bache's team, with a full-width parcel shelf running just below the windscreen and glove boxes repositioned at knee height, with drop-down lids made of plastic which would crush in an accident. The whole dashboard was a single lightweight plastic moulding, grained to look like leather – Bache has said that to get the desired effect he made a dashboard, covered it in leather and had the moulds taken directly from it! Instruments, in typical Bache style, were in a separate 'pod' superimposed on the parcel shelf and consisted of a fashionable strip-type

speedometer, plus petrol and water temperature gauges, with all other functions reduced to warning lights in a row across the top. Switchgear was carefully laid out along the edge of the parcel shelf, with switches of different shapes to aid identification. A central console carried trinket trays and provision for a radio, while the handbrake moved back to its pre-P4 position on the transmission tunnel.

The first interior change was the addition of a steady prop to the rear view mirror in late 1964. Later in the 1965 model-year, the mirror support was fitted with a courtesy light to replace the rather temperamental lights fitted at the dashboard ends on early cars. This courtesy light in turn disappeared along with the interior light over the rear window when a centrally-mounted roof lamp arrived with the Three Thousand Five models in 1968, although the rear-mounted light was retained when a sunroof was fitted.

Front and rear headrests could be supplied from 1965, those on the front requiring a revised seat back with internal mounting brackets, which was later standardized, and bar-type front seat adjusters replaced the cable-operated type towards the end of 1967. Meanwhile, a 120mph speedometer had replaced the 115mph original with the introduction of the TC cars in 1966, and there had been new knobs for the heater, choke and petrol reserve controls. The TC itself had a rev-counter and a resited clock, and this facia change became optional for other models. Early TCs had a 'TC' badge on the radio speaker panel and a further TC-related option was an imitation-wood-rimmed steering wheel with a matching wooden gear lever knob.

The only interior changes made for the Three Thousand Five were a 140mph speedometer with a black instead of chromed bezel, a 'V8' badge on the radio speaker panel and a '3500' badge on the steering wheel, but major changes came with the North American 3500S. Some of these were later standardized on Mk II models, like the instrument layout with four round dials instead of a rectangular box, new internally-illuminated switchgear, non-adjustable front seat head restraints, bigger front door armrests and turnwheel-operated front quarter-lights. The standard seats anticipated the manual transmission 3500S by being covered in the perforated vinyl known as Ambla, and having

box-pleating which David Bache has said was originally designed for the aborted P8 saloon. Leather was an option not often specified, although all the cars did have a leather-covered steering wheel rim. Air conditioning, which brought with it Sundym glass, was a commonly-specified option. Many 3500S items would never reach the home market cars, however. Thus the boot area was far more comprehensively carpeted than that of the Mk II models (the Denovo-shod cars excepted), and there were electric window lifts, a colour-keyed console panel and handbrake gaiter, and rigid map pockets beneath the front door armrests.The Mk II models' interiors varied rather more than the Mk Is'. Even though all of them had the new front armrests, turnwheel-operated quarter-lights, and darker 'wood' trim, only the 2000TC and V8-engined cars had the new switchgear and the new instrument panel with its round dials. Box-pleated Ambla upholstery was an uncommon 2000SC-only option, and brushed nylon seat facings could be had in Sandalwood (Ebony soon became available, and Bronze replaced Sandalwood for 1973). Ambla upholstery was standardized on the manual-transmission 3500S in order to keep this model's base-price below that of its automatic equivalent, although leather remained available as an extra-cost option.

The next round of revisions coincided with the introduction of the 2200 models for the 1974 season. All three manual-gearbox cars had a longer gear lever, while non-adjustable front seat head restraints were standardized on both V8-engined models; first seen on the North American 3500S, these were optionally available on 2200s. All models lost the parking lights switch, and the 3500S lost its Ambla upholstery. All across the range, seats were henceforth to a box-pleated pattern, and leather was relegated to an option in place of the standard corded brushed-nylon coverings. Front seats also had modified backrests to give more legroom in the rear (and, unintentionally, less comfort in the front), while there was a new convex rear-view mirror on a collapsible safety stem, with reshaped sun visors to fit round it. Shortly after the 2200's introduction, a cheaper tufted carpet material available in brown only was used on all models, but the only subsequent

changes were made for the limited-edition 3500 'VIP' models, which had SD1-type seat fabric and headlining and 3500S Automatic-type air conditioning as standard.

Special-bodied P6s were, of course, limited in number because of the relative inflexibility of the base-unit structure. The earliest conversion was carried out in 1965 by FLM Panelcraft on Peter Wilks' instructions. This was a two-door convertible based on a standard 2000 and had actually been inspired by Panelcraft's 1964 P5 convertible for a private customer which Wilks had inspected. Panelcraft also built an estate prototype from a 2000 in 1966. Meanwhile, Rover commissioned the Italian coachbuilder Zagato to build a two-door fastback coupe from a 1965 2000S (twin-carburettor), and David Bache designed his own two-door fastback on a 3500 base-unit in 1966-67, which would probably have worn the badge of Rover's Alvis subsidiary if it had ever gone into production. The mid-1960s also saw at least three 'specials' built by the Swiss coachbuilder Graber. These included a 2000 two-door convertible in 1966, a 2000TC two-door coupe the following year, and a 3500 two-door coupe in 1968.

It was principally the British Leyland takeover in 1967 which killed off production prospects for the Rover-commissioned 'specials', but the estate car variant *was* built in limited numbers, albeit as an aftermarket conversion by FLM Panelcraft, not a production model by Rover. Briefly known as the Panelcraft Estoura, the car was at first marketed exclusively by Crayford Auto Development (and these cars bear a Crayford badge), then by Hurst Park Automobiles of East Molesey, Surrey, and after 1970 by H.R. Owen, when it became known rather misleadingly as the 'Owen conversion'. Conversions were available on used as well as new cars and after 1968, a 3500 version could be obtained. The 2000 and 2000TC estates remained rare because they were too expensive for a market already well covered by Triumph's 2000 estate. The 3500 estate was a success, however, and before production stopped in 1976, a few 3500S estates with manual transmission had been built.

Exact figures are not available, but it seems that between 150 and 160 P6 estates were built. There were some minor

FLM Panelcraft's estate conversion on P6 models offered 49.5 cubic feet of load space.

variations over the years, the most significant being the addition on H.R. Owen cars of an electric fuel pump in place of the mechanical one to overcome airlock problems with the special fuel tanks fitted to the estates. Even though load-carrying space in the cars was limited by a sloping roofline, which also hindered rearward visibility, the 3500 versions sold tolerably well for a few years to the sort of customer who was prepared to pay just a little extra to get something out of the ordinary.

If the professional classes who had always formed the core of Rover's clientele accepted the P6 as a quality car in the Rover tradition, they were not fooled into thinking it shared the exclusivity of its forebears – the sheer numbers in which it was produced saw to that. Although Solihull had allowed plant capacity initially for 500 cars a week (maximum production volume of the P4 had been around 280 cars a week in the 1954 model year), it rapidly became clear that this was not enough. A series of industrial disputes in the mid-1960s ensured a permanent waiting list for the standard car, and this must have discouraged attempts to put rebodied versions into production. In the middle of 1972, Solihull was finally able to increase production targets to 1,000 cars per week; by this stage, customers were having to wait four to six months for a 3500S, although delivery times for the 2000 models were rather shorter. Over 329,000 P6s were built – the exact total is in dispute – huge volumes by Rover standards, but tiny compared to British Leyland's rosy vision of production figures for the P6's successor, the SD1.

CHAPTER 7

Racing and rallying Rovers

Competition cars and prototypes

Although a number of 'specials' based on Rover mechanical parts were built by enthusiasts for trials and club racing in the years immediately after the war, undoubtedly the best-known was the Rover Special built for their own amusement by three of Rover's young engineers, Spen King, Peter Wilks and George Mackie. No-one could deny that the car had a distinguished career in club racing in its early years and, indeed, it continues to perform well in Historic racing events at the time of writing. Nevertheless, even greater interest attaches to its mechanical development over the years. Since it was built in 1948, the car has used a number of fascinating cast-off Rover prototype components and has also indirectly served as a test-bed for many of the ideas which King and Wilks put into Rover production cars of the 1950s and 1960s.

The car's first successes in 1949 attracted a limited amount of official approval from the Rover Company, but it always remained essentially a private venture, and until they became too deeply involved with the Marauder project, King, Wilks and Mackie raced it themselves. They were joined during 1949 by Jack Gethin, of the Birmingham Rover distributors, who took his turn at the wheel and provided in return both finance and workshop space. It was Gethin's firm which Peter Wilks would later join before returning to Rover after the failure of his own Marauder Car Company. Although other drivers used the car during the 1950s, it remained the property of its original owners until some time in the late 1960s, when it was sold to Frank Lockhart, its regular driver since 1963. Needless to say,

King, Wilks and Mackie always retained a fatherly interest in their 'baby'!

The chassis of the Rover Special was the prototype of what became the P3 chassis, designed just before the war by Adrian Lombard. The car also had prototype P3 IFS, and a four-cylinder prototype IOE engine of around 1.2 litres. By the time Rover agreed to part with it, it had already covered some 110,000 miles, having run throughout the war in a Rover 10! King, Wilks and Mackie shortened the chassis, fitted quarter-elliptic springs at the rear and lowered the front suspension, changed the axle ratio and added a single-seater body made by John Griffiths, which has subsequently been altered very little. Total weight was around 14cwt.

The car was first raced with its original engine bored out to 1.5 litres, but for the 1949 season it was given a discarded prototype 2,103cc P3 engine, which was sleeved down to 1,996cc (with a bore of 63.5mm) in order to get under the 2-litre barrier in force for Formula 2 events. Power was boosted by the use of triple SU carburettors, on a manifold similar to that seen on the triple-SU P3 75 cars and later on the Marauder 100, which was of course another Wilks-King-Mackie collaboration. With a compression ratio of 12:1, the engine was prone to head gasket failures, and an intriguing system of bolts was devised to ensure that the head stayed on. Inevitably, by this time Jack Swaine was helping out on engine development! The Rover gearbox – also said to have been a prototype – was discarded at the same time in favour of an ENV preselector unit of the type then familiar on the

These two photographs show the Rover Special as it was in 1982. The P3-type IFS can be seen in the front view.

racing circuits.

Axle development continued during 1949, and the differential was removed in order to obtain better sprint times. More significant, however, was the fitting in the winter of 1949 of a De Dion axle, still without a differential. Experience with this axle/suspension layout in the Rover Special led Spen King and Peter Wilks many years later to go for a De Dion rear end in the P6, and of course King's T3 gas turbine car and the P6BS coupe used De Dion

layouts. It is no coincidence, either, that the P6 had inboard disc brakes to reduce unsprung weight, as the Rover Special employed inboard brakes – albeit drums – for precisely the same reason.

In 1950, a prototype P4 90 engine was acquired for the car. It was simply an over-bored 75 unit of the type tried experimentally before the 'spread-bore' design was adopted. A special short-throw (78.75mm) crankshaft was ordered from Laystall and fitted, so that the capacity would still be under 2 litres. The 1,993cc engine was run on the test-bed with six Amal carburettors, but as most of the owners' enthusiasm and spare time was by now going into the Marauder venture, the engine was never actually put into the car.

Gerry Dunham (of Dunham and Haines, the Luton Rover agents) drove the car in some International events during the early 1950s, and these qualified it for the Historic section of VSCC events in which it now competes. Dunham replaced the 1,996cc engine with a P4 75 unit bored out to 2.4 litres, which was almost certainly in fact a Marauder 100 2,390cc engine, but by the time Frank Lockhart took over the Special in 1963, the 1,993cc engine was in the car. Unfortunately, the special crankshaft wrecked itself two years later, and at Spen King's suggestion an early 75 crank went in with 90 pistons to give the 2,638cc of the original prototype engine. A compression ratio of 9:1 was higher than the original, however. This engine ran its bearings in 1968, and was temporarily replaced by a P5 3-litre unit, wearing another triple-carburettor manifold – this time the prototype designed by Raymond Mays for the 3-litre several years earlier! Yet another engine swop took place in 1977, when a 2.6-litre unit was installed, again with the Mays manifold. An errant con-rod bolt wrote off this engine the following year, and so the earlier 2,638cc engine was rebuilt and reinstalled, fitted with the original (1949) triple-carburettor manifold. Thus the car remains today.

The Rover Special, of course, was rather separate from the mainstream of Rover engineering and policy. The Company did not actually put together a works team for serious competition in motor sport until the early 1960s, although they had sponsored several factory entries in the genteel British concours and long-distance road rallies of the 1930s.

Rover's Competitions Department was William Martin-Hurst's idea. Promoted in 1960 from Production Director to Managing Director, he set about preparing the way for the new image which the Company would need for the 1960s and beyond. Primarily, that new image was all to do with the Rover 2000, which was still a long way from its launch date, and somehow the existing cars had to be made into heralds of this new high-performance vehicle. The answer seemed to Martin-Hurst to lie in entering Rovers for motor sport – not circuit-racing, of course, but long-distance rallying of the type which would best show up the durability, reliability and high-speed cruising ability of the Company's newest product, the P5 3-litre.

The first step was to take a 3-litre to Africa and to hammer it up and down the continent for 15,000 miles in an extensive three-month tryout. This was followed by further testing at the Fighting Vehicle Research and Development Establishment at Bagshot, Surrey. The Board agreed that

One of the original 3-litre rally cars displays its competition equipment for the 1962 East African Safari. The door trim identifies this as a Mk IA model, and therefore as one of the locally-prepared cars.

677 DNX during the 1963 East African Safari, in which it was the only Rover to finish.

4 KUE was the car which took Roger Clark and Jim Porter to sixth place in the 1965 Monte Carlo Rally. It is seen here on the RAC Rally in 1964.

Martin-Hurst could go ahead with the 3-litre cars as rally entrants, but there was some initial caution about the enterprise: Rover simply gave official support to the first appearance of the 3-litres in rallying, and the team was actually entered for the East African Safari Rally in April 1962 by the Company's East African distributors, the Cooper Motor Corporation. Not until the cars had proved that they had some chance did Solihull set up its own Competitions Department, which was established with Ralph Nash at its head in July 1962. Nash continued to fulfil his duties as superintendent of the engineering workshops as well until Jim Porter assumed control of the Competitions Department during 1965 and he was able to return to his former job full-time. Although Nash knew nothing about rally-driving, he was fortunate in securing as his second-in-command Tony Cox, who did at least have experience of club rallying, and he was also able to assemble a team of expert mechanics from within his own department.

The object of the exercise was defined right from the start as being that the cars should finish — nobody expected them

to win — and preparation was accordingly designed to keep them going at all costs. Nevertheless, when the engines were being blueprinted by the Experimental Department, the engineers there could not resist a few little touches like polished exhaust ports and ultra-tough valve springs, just to help things along! Exhausts, of course, were modified to give more bhp, and wiring (although not brake piping) was routed through the passenger compartment to make service attention easier.

There were actually two-and-a-half teams of 3-litre rally cars, the half a team being two of the four cars entered for the 1962 Safari which had been prepared locally, not by Solihull. Nevertheless, all four of the cars which would later form the first Rover team went to East Africa for the 1962 Safari, the two non-competitors acting as service and back-up vehicles. The problem of tracing which car is which is not made any easier by the fact that all the competing cars had to be registered locally (as KHD 262, 549, 550 and 551); all that can be established for certain is that the four cars which formed the team after this first rally had consecutive commission numbers in the Mk II series, and were then registered 676-679 DNX in July or August 1962.

Generally speaking, the Rover team drivers kept to one regular car, although the issue is complicated by the number of changes there were in that team of drivers! In the 1962 Safari, three of the cars were driven by local crews, but subsequently 676 DNX was normally driven by Johnny Cuff with John Howarth or John Baguley, 677 DNX was Bill Bengry's car and was shared with David Skeffington, 679 DNX belonged to Ken James and Mike Hughes, and 678 DNX was the 'guest driver' car, being piloted by Peter Riviere and Ronnie Adams and then Raymond Baxter and Ernest McMillan. In the summer of 1963, the DNX-registered cars were relegated to a second-division team, and put in regular appearances either as practice or service back-up vehicles, or as privately-entered cars prepared by the factory. 676 DNX was sold in October 1963 to Richard Martin-Hurst, the son of Rover's Managing Director, and was actively campaigned by him alongside the works team cars. 677 DNX was written off in a fairly spectacular accident during the 1964 Monte Carlo Rally, but the other two cars were still going strong as late as 1965, when they were driven by Army teams in the Scottish International Rally. Both were scrapped early in 1967, but the eventual fate of 676 DNX is unknown.

If the 3-litres did not exactly set the rallying world alight by their performance in the 1962 Safari, they did astound the motoring world by their reliability. Although two of the cars were put out of the running by accidents, the other two gained third and fifth places in the over-2,500cc class, coming 25th and 31st overall out of the 45 finishers (109 cars had started). Both were crewed by local teams, and an internal memorandum at Solihull made much of the comment from the Vincent father-and-son crew that the only problem they had encountered on their way to third place was when the car's cigar lighter had failed to function! The next rally in which the Rovers performed was the Liège-Sofia-Liège in the autumn, when all four DNX-registered cars ran as private entries prepared by the Rover Competitions Department. Two cars were eliminated by

Two competition cars were built with long-stroke V8 engines. JXC 808D was the first of these and it still exists, in private ownership.

accidents, Bill Bengry and David Skeffington came 18th and last of the 100 entrants to finish, but Ken James and Mike Hughes scored a magnificent class win, coming sixth overall. The same crew took 679 DNX to third place in the over-1,600cc Touring class and an 11th overall placing in the RAC Rally that winter, while the works cars as a whole took third place in the Manufacturer's Team Award. The DNX cars put in their last rallying appearance on Rover's behalf as a team for the East African Safari of April 1963. This proved to be an extraordinarily tough event and three of the cars were eliminated by accidents, but Bill Bengry and local driver G.E.Goby, who had piloted a 3-litre in the previous year's event, finished seventh and last of the 84 starters, gaining first place in their class. Not that there was much competition; they were the only large car to finish!

Meanwhile, the Competitions Department was preparing a second team of four 3-litres, this time Mk IIB models, but apparently fitted with the 'big crank' engine then under development for autumn 1964 introduction. These were registered in June as 996-999 GNX. 999 GNX was regularly crewed by Ken James and Mike Hughes, 997 GNX by Bill Bengry and Barry Hughes until they left Rover at the close

The 4.3-litre V8 racing engine.

of the 1963 rallying season, and the other two cars were driven variously by Johnny Cuff and Norman Baguley, Willie Cave and John Sprinzel or the Competitions Department's foreman Tony Cox, Ann Hall and Peter Riley, and Logan Morrison with Johnstone Syer. Their last appearance in the Rover team was in the 1964 Spa-Sofia-Liège, although private entrants used them in a number of rallies after that date. 999 GNX was sold to a dealer in May 1966 and its subsequent history is unknown, but the other three cars were broken up in April the following year.

Only 20 cars finished of the 120 entrants for the Liège-Sofia-Liège Rally of August 1963, and two of the four works-entered 3-litres were put out by accidents. Ken James and Mike Hughes, however, achieved a class win and eighth place overall, while Bill Bengry and Barry Hughes took third place in the over-2,000cc class and 18th overall position. Five cars were entered for the RAC Rally in November, the four works cars including one of the older DNX vehicles, and the fifth entry being Tony Cox in the privately-prepared 998 GNX. As a publicity gimmick, the cars were entered without a service back-up, and expectations were not disappointed; all five finished, taking in addition third, fourth and fifth places in their class and coming third in the Manufacturer's Team Award.

1964 started off less well with two private entries in the Monte Carlo Rally, one of which went out after an accident, while Ken James and Mike Hughes finished the road section without loss of points, but were heavily penalized on the special stages, ending up 69th overall. Two of the four team entries finished the Acropolis Rally in May, with James and Hughes taking sixth overall and second in class, followed by Tony Cox and Willie Cave with 11th overall and fourth in class. Between them, with third position in the class and ninth overall placing, was the privately-entered 676 DNX of Richard Martin-Hurst, whose co-driver was the then barely-known Roger Clark. No 3-litres went in for the Alpine Rally in June, which was given over to the first competition appearance of the 2000s, and none of the Rovers – of which three were 3-litres, two entered by the works – finished in the Spa-Sofia-Liège later that year.

The 2000 was so much more obviously suited to competition work than the 3-litre that it was inevitable it should succeed the older model in the Rover team. Four 2000s were initially prepared at Solihull, but 1 KUE to 4 KUE were later to be joined by a variety of other cars which were technically privately-owned, even though they had been registered at Solihull. Most of these bore the XC registrations commonly found on Rover Company vehicles at the time, although an exception was 151 FLK, a very early 2000 with a registration number following on from the pre-production cars, which was campaigned by Tony Cox. From the start, two of the KUE cars ran prototype 2000TC engines, and eventually all the cars were TC-equipped.

Only two of the four works 2000s finished in their first rally, Ken James and Mike Hughes in a TC taking third in their class and ninth in the Grand Touring category, while Peter Riley's standard car achieved a third in class and fifth place in the Touring category. None of the 2000s finished in the Spa-Sofia-Liège, but Anne Hall and Pat Spencer managed a 16th overall plus third in the Ladies' section of the RAC Rally that November. All this was scarcely an auspicious start to the 2000s' competition career, but fortunately all was redeemed by Roger Clark's amazing performance in the 1965 Monte Carlo Rally when, driving 4 KUE with Jim Porter, he took a class win, first in the Production Touring Cars category and sixth place overall. In the excitement, nobody seemed to care that the other three works 2000s had failed to finish. Clark himself became an overnight star, and of course left Rover after the 1965 rallying season to go on to even greater things. Although the works 2000s put up some good performances subsequently, they were never to equal the 1965 Monte Carlo Rally success.

During 1965, the number of rallying 2000s proliferated. There were private entries prepared at Solihull in the Circuit of Ireland, the Welsh International Rally, the RAC Rally and the Scottish International Rally, with placings achieved by Logan Morrison and Johnstone Syer in the last-named (a class win and third overall), and by Tony Cox and David Fawcett in the Welsh event (third in class and 12th overall). Chris Knowles-Fitton and C.G.Nash also finished in this latter rally, in 32nd place overall. The works team entries were limited to the Acropolis, Alpine and RAC Rallies, and although none of the cars finished in the first of these, the results obtained in the other two enabled Rover to continue holding their heads high. In the Alpine Rally, Andrew Cowan and Brian Coyle came third overall and first in the Grand Touring category with a 2000TC, while of the standard cars, that driven by Roger Clark and Jim Porter claimed 10th overall and fourth in the Touring category, with Logan Morrison and Johnstone Syer in 16th place overall and fifth in the Touring category. Anne Hall and Pat Spencer achieved 22nd place overall and sixth in the

Le Mans in 1965, with the Rover-BRM gas turbine sports/racer in its final form.

Touring category, even after an unplanned excursion over a 40-foot slope near the end. Clark and Porter came 14th overall in the RAC Rally and were second in their class, while Morrison and Syer finished 17th overall and took third place in their class.

Rover announced a four-rally programme for 1966 – the Monte Carlo, Acropolis, Alpine and RAC events – with the possibility of supporting private entries in the Circuit of Ireland and Scottish International events. They duly sponsored the seven Rovers entered for the Monte Carlo in which, after a squabble over modifications which led to the Ford and BMC cars being disqualified, Jim Porter and Geoffrey Mabbs came 10th overall with the wire-wheeled TC registered JXC 8C – but then they pulled out of motor sport altogether. The ostensible reason was disenchantment after the Monte Carlo disqualification fiasco (although Rover's own cars had not been affected); the reason given to the public was the pressing need to devote the Engineering Department's time more fully to other commitments; but in fact it was becoming increasingly apparent at Solihull that in order to remain competitive in rallying it would be necessary to start thinking in terms of very much modified engines and lightweight bodyshells, and this was not what the Rover teams had been all about. Although the withdrawal was touted as 'temporary', the Competitions Department closed down for good. The fate of the rallying 2000s is not clear, although 4 KUE passed into the hands of Brian Terry, an engineer in the Experimental Department, who eventually resold it. Before letting it out of their sight, however, Rover had disguised the car by respraying it in white (it was originally Copperleaf Red) and, because Ralph Nash wanted to keep all the famous KUE registration plates, 4 KUE was reregistered as JXC 226C.

The closure of the Competitions Department was not the end of Rovers in competition, however. Four years later, Peter Browning, British Leyland's Competitions Manager, chose to campaign a Rover 3500 for the 1970 season and, despite both scepticism and obstruction from the Rover management, he was able – with Ralph Nash's help – to secure JXC 808D, which had started life in 1966 as one of the V8 development cars.

Development was carried out on behalf of BL by Roy Pierpoint and Bill Shaw, who fitted the car with a 4.3-litre Traco-Oldsmobile V8 (essentially a race-tuned version of the GM engine) and gave it a new lightweight racing body with flared wings and wheelarches. With four Weber carburettors the power output was 360bhp at 6,800rpm, so not surprisingly the standard Rover 2000 gearbox (mated to a Jaguar E-type differential) let the car down on more than one occasion! An American Muncie gearbox was then fitted, and in the hands of Roy Pierpoint the car had a relatively successful season in club racing, its major success being first place in the 100-miles Saloon Car race at Silverstone.

JXC 808D was then sold off (and it still exists, in restored form) and work began on a Group 6 prototype car, initially for racing, but with a view to homologation as a Group 2 rally car. BL had not ruled out the possibility of a limited production run of special-equipment V8s, although Solihull management had considerable doubts about the idea! This second car was again the work of Pierpoint and Shaw, who fitted it with a similar big V8 to the first, although this time final development was carried out by BL's Competitions Department at Abingdon. In September 1971, the new car was entered for the 84-hours Marathon de la Route at the Nurburgring. Despite a strict rev limit of 4,500rpm, imposed because the car was relatively untried, the Rover shot away from the rest of the field on the first lap, and by the time it was forced to retire with severe propshaft vibration 16 hours later, it had an amazing three-lap lead over the rest of the field, headed by the works Porsches! Sadly, BL closed the Competitions Department before the car was able to prove its worth in any more races. Much later, Rovers would again fly the BL flag when the BL Motorsport Division's racing SD1s trounced the Ford opposition in the 1981 British Saloon Car Championship.

Rover's competition cars were not all based on production saloons, however, and William Martin-Hurst's enthusiasm for motor sport underpinned another venture in the early 1960s. In 1962, the Automobile Club de l'Ouest had invited the T4 gas turbine car to make a demonstration run at the Le Mans circuit and had announced at the same time that they would offer a prize for the first gas turbine car to average 150kph (about 93mph) or more during the Le Mans 24-hours race.

Martin-Hurst seized on this opportunity and started looking for ways of making a Rover gas turbine sports/racing car. Realizing that it was too much for Solihull to attempt alone, he approached John Cooper with a view to collaboration. The racing car builder rejected the idea, so Martin-Hurst next contacted Sir Alfred Owen, whose BRM cars had had a magnificent 1962 season, taking Graham Hill to a World Championship. Owen at once agreed to the venture and a 1962 Grand Prix BRM was duly stripped of its single-seater body, subjected to major surgery of its spaceframe and given a 150bhp rear-mounted Rover gas turbine engine, type 2S/150/R. A two-seat sports/racing body was hastily fabricated by Motor Bodies, another of Owen's concerns, and BRM provided their regular drivers, Graham Hill and Richie Ginther, for the first appearance of the Rover-BRM at Le Mans. In practice sessions during April 1963 the car lapped at 111.24mph; in the actual race in June, it averaged 107.84mph for the 24 hours, which would have put it in eighth place overall had the regulations permitted it to compete with the other cars.

David Bache's Styling Department voiced strong dissatisfaction with the ugly body shape and were given the go-ahead to design a more aerodynamic one for the 1964 race. New regulations meant that the car could now compete, rated at 1,992cc, but unfortunately it suffered severe damage when it fell from its trailer on the way back from practice sessions at Le Mans that April. It was withdrawn from the 1964 race with the excuse that the heat-exchangers being developed for the engine were not ready – which, of course, was only half the truth! By the time it resurfaced the following year, the new body had been further altered by the addition of huge ram-air intakes ahead of the rear wheels to aid engine-bay cooling. The rear suspension had also been changed and, of course, the heat-exchangers were now fitted.

The car ran in the 1965 Le Mans race, driven again by Graham Hill with the new BRM driver Jackie Stewart. Unfortunately, a foreign body found its way into the engine, causing it to overheat, and 10th place overall with an average speed of 98.8mph was the best that could be achieved. It did, however, score a historic 'first' as the first gas turbine car to compete in and finish a motor race, and it was awarded the *Motor* magazine trophy for the highest-placed British entrant. A fuel consumption of 13.5mpg, as compared to the 7mpg achieved at the 1963 Le Mans, showed that the heat-exchangers were doing their work, but by now enthusiasm for gas turbine engines was on the wane at Solihull. The closure of the Competitions Department in 1966 signalled the end of Rover's involvement with motor sport, and the Rover-BRM never raced again. It is now part of the BL Heritage collection.

Stillborn prototypes

M-Type
Towards the end of the Second World War, it seemed clear to Spencer Wilks that in the economic depression which was bound to follow, demand for the medium-sized cars which were Rover's stock-in-trade would fall off and be replaced by a demand for cheaper, smaller cars. To ensure the Company's long-term survival, therefore, he had approved a plan to produce a 6hp car. Prototypes of the M-type (M for Miniature) were built and tested in 1945-46, but the car never saw production. The Government emphasis on medium-sized cars as desirable exports, their one-maker/one-model policy, and above all their change to a flat-rate motor taxation system, all conspired to kill it off.

The baby Rover, designed by Gordon Bashford with styling by Harry Loker under Maurice Wilks' guidance, sat on a 77in wheelbase, and was powered by a 28bhp 699cc version of the four-cylinder IOE engine. Steel shortages had been foreseen and both the platform-chassis and the body were therefore fabricated from light alloy. Despite its small size, the car was a full four-seater, capable of around 60mph. Performance and handling were good and the vehicle could have been every bit as good as the early Morris Minor, although it must be admitted that styling was rather less successful, the body having heavy rear quarters and being scaled-down rather unhappily from the 1942 season American idiom. The front grille and headlamp arrangement was echoed on early clay models for both the P2 and P4.

Although an open version was under consideration, the three prototypes all had two-door closed bodies. One of them survived into the 1960s in the hands of Jess Worster, Director of Rover's Tyseley Works, and an engine has since been discovered and preserved for the BL Heritage collection.

Road Rover

The Road Rover was always an odd project in that its precise purpose never seemed to be clearly defined. It grew originally out of the Land-Rover as a rather more refined two-wheel-drive variant of the station wagon, using a P4 car chassis. The first prototype was built in 1952 and was christened 'The Greenhouse' because of its basic, Land-Rover-derived styling. Several more prototypes to similar specification were built until a rethink in 1955 attacked the problem from the other end, as it were, and redefined the aim as a rugged two-wheel-drive estate car, closer in concept to the cars than to the Land-Rover. With a completely new

The M-type was a baby car which would have been built to traditional Rover standards of quality.

MWD 716 was one of the first series of Road Rover prototypes, and is similar to the vehicle now owned by BL Heritage.

T3, the four-wheel-drive gas turbine coupe, is now preserved by BL Heritage.

body, based heavily on contemporary Chevrolet styling and apparently using some saloon car parts, the first Series 2 Road Rover was built in spring 1956. Like the earlier prototypes, this had a modified P4 car chassis and a 1,997cc P4 60 engine, but later cars in the prototype series had the 2,286cc Land-Rover petrol engine.

Production plans were ambitious; besides the basic two-door Station Wagon, a two-door Saloon, a Van and a Pickup with either cab or canvas hood were drawn up, and work began on a four-door Station Wagon. Production was scheduled to begin in early 1958, but was put off until autumn 1959, then July 1960, and finally the Road Rover project collapsed about the middle of 1959. No-one quite knows why, but it seems probable that there were three main factors – the whole project had become over-complicated, the exact sales area had still not been fully defined, and Solihull had quite enough other work to do on the P6 project. Several years later, the Road Rover concept would re-emerge in a much-refined form as the Range Rover.

T3

The T3 was actually the fourth gas turbine prototype, and

was the first such Rover not to use a production body/chassis structure. Based on a box-section chassis-frame with a 94in wheelbase, it had a two-door, two-seater, fixed-head coupe body made of glass-reinforced polyester resin with local steel reinforcing members inserted at the moulding stage.

Following the exhaust gas dispersal problems encountered with the front-engined T2, the 2S/100 turbine engine was mounted at the rear. It produced around 110bhp to give this $19\frac{1}{4}$cwt car a top speed in the region of 115mph. The transmission dispensed with the T2A's conventional gearbox and reverted to the JET 1 pattern in which the engine performed the function of a torque convertor, so that all the driving could be done on a single ratio. A simple change lever selected reverse, which had exactly the same gearing as forward.

Chassis engineering was by Spen King and incorporated many of the ideas which he and Gordon Bashford would later put into the P6. The rear suspension was a De Dion layout with fixed-length drive-shafts and a Watt linkage, a sliding-joint arrangement being employed to take care of variations in track. Inboard Dunlop disc brakes were fitted front and rear, with rack-and-pinion steering and coil-spring-

This styling studio mock-up shows the impressive lines of the big P8 saloon. Just visible behind is a Range Rover styling buck.

and-wishbone independent front suspension. To aid traction and roadholding, a four-wheel drive layout was used.

The T3, as a bodyless test-bed, began testing on January 16, 1956. It first ran as a complete car at MIRA on September 16, and was displayed at the London Motor Show later that year, although there was never any intention

The roadgoing P8 ptototypes were badged as 'Mantelays' to confuse industry and press spies. Photograph by Alan Milstead; badge from the Geoff Kent Collection.

The P6BS ptototype, with the P9 styling model proposed by David Bache's team. Although the car would probably have become an Alvis, it bears Rover badging here. There are still many who bitterly regret that it never went into production.

The P10 as a scale mock-up. The 'shadow' around the roof and wind-screen is an alternative outline; like many mock-ups, this one presented different proposals on its two sides. The general outline of what would become SD1 is already apparent.

that it should become a production model. It remained a development car for a number of years – work concentrating on the heat-exchangers Rover hoped would reduce the high fuel consumption which handicapped all the gas turbine cars – and it is now retained by BL Heritage.

P6BS/P9

The P6BS owed its inception to the exciting possibilites which the ex-Buick V8 engine opened up in the mid-1960s, and indirectly to William Martin-Hurst's enthusiasm for sporting cars and the success of the Rover-BRM gas turbine car. Quite different from the normal run of Rover projects, it was a mid-engined three-seater sports car drawn up by Spen King and Gordon Bashford, using an all-steel welded body and a number of P6 running components, hence its P6 designation, plus B for Buick and S for Sports.

The heart of the design was a Buick V8 engine, modified with parts from its Rover derivative and fitted with big 2in SUs to give around 185bhp. Mounted back-to-front and offset slightly to the right, it left room for a third passenger seat alongside. Drive was taken through a four-speed gearbox to the rear wheels, which had a semi-independent De Dion setup. The car's light weight, low build and wide track allied to the mid-engined layout gave staggeringly good roadholding and handling and top speed was in the region of

140mph. Without a doubt, production cars could have been even faster, and the use of P6 running gear convinced Rover that the car could have been sold very cheaply indeed.

NMT 396E was built up during 1966 and registered for road use in the early part of 1967. Early plans had been to put it into production under the badge of Rover's Alvis subsidiary and most of the testing of the prototype was done by Alvis. By 1968, however, it was clear that the car would not go into production and British Leyland management lent it out to various motoring journals for road-test as an interesting might-have-been. The overwhelmingly enthusiastic reviews which these magazines printed may well have been a factor in the 1969 decision to reconsider the car for production. As the chunky, functional body style with its simple single-curvature panels had never been intended by Bashford and King as a production design, David Bache's styling team were instructed to redraw the car. The project had got as far as a full-size mock-up when Jaguar's Sir William Lyons heard about it. When he learned that Rover intended to sell this new P9 at several hundred pounds below the cost of an E-type, he used all the influence he had on the British Leyland Board to get the project killed off. Less than two years later, he would do the same to ensure that the P8 did not spoil the market for Jaguar's XJ saloons; sadly, Rover had no representative on the British Leyland

119

In addition to the V8, the P10 would have had a DOHC slant-four engine of 2.2 litres. One of the prototypes, fitted with fuel injection, is preserved by BL Heritage.

Board who commanded the same respect as Sir William.

Although an early picture of the P6BS being built in the jig shop at Solihull shows it with Rostyle wheels, it was fitted with Minilites when Rover lent it to the motoring journals. The Rover 2000 wheels and hubcaps with which it has latterly been seen scarcely do justice to the design, and one is tempted to suspect that their fitting may have been intended to detract from the appeal of a vehicle which should, without any doubt, have been built. The unique prototype now forms part of the BL Heritage collection, where it is kept company by a splendid one-eighth scale model of the Bache-designed P9.

P8

The P8 was the second of the two major disappointments in Rover's history after the British Leyland takeover. It had first begun to take shape in 1963 as a luxury-market successor to the P5; design work had become very serious two years later when the V8 engine became available, and the British Leyland Board gave it the go-ahead in 1968. From the first, the P8 had been conceived as a Mercedes-eater, but it gradually became apparent that it would also be a Jaguar-eater. As British Leyland were unwilling to risk a head-on clash between the two marques the Rover had to go. So go it did, in March 1971, less than six months before its scheduled launch date and after millions of pounds had already been spent on production tooling.

Few people would disagree that Sir William Lyons' XJ saloon was a much more graceful creation than David Bache's heavy, chunky P8, but the Rover design certainly had an impressive appearance and would no doubt have been tidied up for production. At one stage, gullwing doors had been seriously considered, but the final design approved for production was a conventional four-door saloon. Basic and detail design were settled in 1968, but by the time the first prototypes were built in 1970 the car had become larger and heavier than its progenitor Spen King would have wished. By then, of course, he had been spirited away to look after the Triumph operation.

The P8 used a base-unit structure generally similar to that of the P6, to which light-alloy skin panels were attached. It had a 108½in wheelbase, with a coil-spring De Dion rear suspension incorporating self-levelling struts, which represented a refinement of the P6 layout. The front suspension was of double-wishbone type, mounted on a tubular subframe which could move fore-and-aft on rods running through the tubes and was bolted at the front to a body crossmember and at the rear to the member carrying the wishbone link pivots. Power-assisted rack-and-pinion steering was to be standard, together with full-power high-pressure disc braking.

The model line-up and model names chosen remain unclear, but three of the six prototypes ran a 4.4-litre V8 engine mated to automatic transmission, while the other three had the familiar 3.5-litre power unit. A manual gearbox would have been available alongside the automatic option. At least one mock-up was badged as a Rover 4000, and a noteworthy feature of the design was the use of polyurethane impactable bumpers front and rear, which would have been painted in the body colour. Some of the prototypes were later used to test SD1 components, and only one (TXC 160J, which was badged as a Mantelay to mislead the curious) survived unmodified. This automatic-transmission car, which was regrettably vandalized while in store at Longbridge, is now the property of BL Heritage. Despite the claim in the BL Heritage catalogue that it has a 3,528cc engine, it is in fact believed to be one of the 4.4-litre prototypes.

Interestingly enough, many of the items developed for the P8 reappeared in other Rover models. The box-pleated seating was used in the later P6s, and the general dashboard layout was retained at the insistence of Lord Stokes, then Chairman of British Leyland, for the early SD1 models. The controversial skeletal bonnet badge of the first SD1s had been drawn up originally for the P8 (it was also proposed for the P9), and the SD1's 'clover leaf' wheel trim was also first seen on a P8. As for the 4.4-litre engine, it found a home in the Australian Leyland P76 range and in Australian Leyland Terrier trucks.

P10

The P10 was Rover's entry in a design contest between the two components of British Leyland's Specialist Car Division to find a replacement for the P6 Rovers and the Triumph 2000/2500 range. As the P10 had to be a much simpler car than the P8, a proposal for front-wheel drive was rejected early on, although a double-wishbone front suspension like that of the P8 remained in the specification until Spen King, by then in charge of the project, insisted on strut suspension to give more room for the catalytic convertors demanded by US emission-control regulations. The P10 was initially discussed by Rover during the first half of 1969, and by March 1970 it was tentatively envisaged as a four/five-seater four-door saloon and a four-seater two-door sports saloon. David Bache put forward the body styles which competed with Triumph's Puma – and it was the Rover design which was given the go-ahead by Leyland management early in 1971. These original Bache designs were fastbacks, which, of course, were easily adaptable to the hatchback layout with which Solihull had already been toying. In February 1971, the P10 became a joint project with Triumph under the project designation RT 1 (Rover-Triumph No 1), and was renamed SD1 (Specialist Division No 1) two months later. In 1976 it was launched with that designation as the Rover 3500.

The P10 was originally planned at Solihull to have three basic models – a high-line car using the 3,528cc V8 engine, a mid-line model with a twin-carburettor (later fuel-injected) 2.2-litre DOHC 'slant-four' and a low-line model with a single-carburettor version of the DOHC engine. When the P10 became the RT1, the two smaller engines were rescheduled as Triumph units. At first, the 2500 'six' was considered, updated by a belt-driven overhead camshaft, but it soon became apparent that this old Triumph engine (which dated in essentials back to the Standard Vanguard Six of 1961) had very little development life left in it. Consequently, Triumph turned to a completely new design of six-cylinder engine, which emerged in 1977 in the 2300 and 2600 versions of the SD1.

It seems that some of the disused P8 prototypes were used during 1971 for suspension and braking development, but it is not entirely clear whether any P10 prototypes were built. The matter is largely academic, as P10, RT1 and SD1 are in fact all part of the same model's evolution. The earliest known SD1 prototype has an L registration suffix (which means it was registered between August 1, 1971 and July 31, 1972) and at the time of writing it is in store at Solihull.

CHAPTER 8

Buying a Classic Rover

The choice and the examination

At the time of writing, Classic Rover enthusiasm divides itself fairly neatly about the 1950 model year, with the wings-and-running-boards brigade separating out from the slab-sides enthusiasts. The difference is rather more than one of affinity for types of body styling, however. The plain fact is that owners of the older models tend not to use their cars very much – and for good, practical reasons. The majority of P4s, P5s and P6s in enthusiasts' hands are still very much on the road, although as years go by, that dividing line of 1950 will certainly creep forwards. Even now, the number of 'Cyclops' P4s in regular use must be tiny.

The first decision to make in buying a Classic Rover is really, therefore, whether or not the car is to be used regularly. There are those who still run P3 and even earlier models as everyday cars, but for the majority of people this is impractical; cruising speeds of 50-60mph and frantic hunts for spare parts are not calculated to give carefree motoring in the 1980s. However, if a car is to be used on summer weekends only and is intended primarily for fun rather than transport, then the pre-1950 Rovers present a wide choice to the enthusiast.

It goes without saying that high speeds in these cars are out, and that the smaller the engine the slower the car. If the car is to be strictly for fun, however, such considerations should have no relevance whatsoever, and the prospective owner can think in terms of body styles and overall condition as his primary aims.

The rarest pre-1950 Rovers are certainly those with coachbuilt bodies, although they are not always the most desirable as not all coachbuilders were able to create such elegant or durable bodies as the standard Rover-built offerings. Tourers have a rarity value, too (especially on the Speed 14 chassis), and the 1935-36 Streamline bodies are undoubtedly rare, although the odd styling of the Saloon makes its desirability questionable. Next down the line, but in no particular order, are the lovely 10hp Coupes of 1938-40 (525 built), the 20hp models (about 600 built), the 1939-40 Tickford dropheads (a few hundred), the 1934 10hp Sports Saloons (only 50) and the four-light P3 60s (fewer than 400 made). Almost anything on the Speed 14 chassis is desirable, as under 400 were made. The prospective purchaser may also be lucky in finding one of the rare 12s and 14s fitted with optional 'Speed' equipment in the mid-1930s.

By far the majority of cars available will be standard four-light and six-light Saloons, however, and anyone who seriously wants one of the rarer models may well have to spend several years trying to locate one. Appearance excepted, there is little to distinguish four-light and six-light bodies, although there is more room in the latter. The post-1936 bodies (post-1938 on the 10hp) had enclosed boots, while earlier cars had an exposed luggage grid. Heaters were not fitted as standard until 1947, although they were optional extras from autumn 1939 and it is usually possible to fit a heater of some sort to earlier models by using a little ingenuity. The P3 models were the first Rovers to have heater-demister ducting built into the bodywork, and consequently they are better served in this department than earlier models. P3 seats, however, are rather less comfortable than those of earlier cars. As all models had a four-speed gearbox with freewheel, there is scarcely any point in looking specifically for the 1939 and later models with their synchromesh on third and top gears.

From the visual point of view, P4 models all look very similar, although there were actually five distinct body types: the Cyclops (1950-52 model years), the boxed headlight model with sloping boot (1952-54), the boxed headlight model with new boot and rear window (1955-56), the new wing model (1957-58), and the final version with revised bumpers and grille (1959-64). The early cars all had bench front seats covered in plain leather, which are both less comfortable and less durable than the pleated-leather type introduced at the same time as bucket front seats in 1956. Most comfortable are the final design with padded edge-rolls; reclining front seats became available in 1961 and fully-adjustable seats the following year. Bench seats were offered until the demise of the 95 and 110 in 1964. Boot space in all models is limited, but in the pre-1954 cars it is particularly bad and in the Cyclops almost useless because of the spare wheel stowage position. In addition, the radial tyres commonly used on P4s nowadays for reasons of durability, availability and better handling are of a size (185–15) which will not fit into an unmodified spare wheel tray; consequently, spare wheels usually end up in the boot, thus effectively leaving no luggage space at all!

On the performance side, the 60, 75, 80 and 105R are the least accelerative models, while the 100, 105/105S and 110 are the quickest. Driving pleasure may also be influenced by transmission arrangements. Freewheels were standard until 1955, and continued to be available until 1959 as an alternative to overdrive; synchromesh covered third and top only until 1953, when it was extended to second gear as well. The 105R, of course, had automatic transmission.

As for desirability, the 'Cyclops' probably rates as the most interesting P4, principally because of its rarity, but its odd frontal design is not to everyone's taste. There is no doubt, however, that the best all-round bets are the 100 and 105/105S models.

Moving on now to the P5, there is a choice of two body shapes – Saloon and (after 1962) Coupe. Coupe models have less interior room and were not available as six-seaters, while Saloons were available with a bench front seat until the arrival of Mk III models in 1965 (although Mk II manual transmission Saloons could not be fitted with the bench seat). The Mk III seats are probably the most comfortable and were carried over for the 3.5-litre models in 1967. It was possible on Mk III and later Saloons to specify the optional bench rear seat, which gave the car a seating capacity of five. The V8-engined cars have several cosmetic exterior differences, which may or may not appeal to the individual's taste.

Early cars did not have the front disc brakes introduced in 1960, and there is no doubt that pre-Mk II models without the Weslake headed engine were pretty lethargic, especially the automatics. Later 3-litre automatics are not that much more rapid, and tend also to be fuel guzzlers because of the inefficiencies of the transmission. The type 35 gearbox introduced on Mk III models does not help in this respect, although the altered gearing gives the cars rather more restful high-speed cruising. The best transmission to go for on a 3-litre is the four-speed with overdrive gearbox of Mk II/III models, that of Mk I/IA cars being close to its tolerance limit with the 3-litre engine. The V8-engined cars afford no choice of transmission, as all are automatic; they are nevertheless faster and even slightly more economical than the 3-litre. PAS was standardized on all Coupes and then on Saloons after autumn 1964, having been optionally available since 1959. Non-PAS cars, especially those prior to the steering ratio change made with Mk IIb models, have heavy steering.

The rarest P5s are the 2.4-litre and 2.6-litre variants, although the model generally reckoned to be the most desirable is the 3.5-litre Coupe with its combination of good looks and V8 performance. After that, the best model to go for is a manual-transmission Mk II or Mk III 3-litre with PAS. There are, of course, those who would say that the 3-litre loses much of its luxury-car character without automatic transmission. The individaul characteristics of Mk I models gives them an interest value which is heightened by the fact that only small numbers have survived, but they are rather deficient in both performance and handling.

As for the P6, it was always intended as a high-performance saloon and so there can be no doubt that the most desirable model is a 3500S with the V8 engine and manual transmission. Next in line comes the 2000TC, and after that the very early 2000, say prior to 1966, mainly because so few have survived. A rarity is the American-specification 3500S, although the drawback here is that almost all had left-hand drive. Estate cars are also rare, and desirable provided one can live with their shortcomings (poor rearward vision, and fuel supply problems on the pre-H.R. Owen cars). Positively not recommended is the 2000 Automatic, which is slow, noisy and thirsty.

Bodyshells did not change over the years, and the only distinguishing features are badging, wheel trims, side trim strips, vinyl roofs and quarter-panels, and the Mk II bonnet. Mk I V8 models had a heavy stainless-steel strip across the leading edge of the bonnet, which makes them look aggressive but is not to everyone's liking. Mk II models had much improved instrumentation (the single-carburettor cars excepted). Seating, for four only, was always in leather until the 3500S appeared with Ambla in 1971; from autumn 1973 leather was relegated to an option in place of the standard nylon cloth.

Having decided on the model that is wanted, the next stage is to go out and find it. At this point, disappointment and disillusionment are likely to set in, as the cars on offer are usually suffering from a variety of unpleasant maladies (otherwise why would their owners part with them?). The wise would-be owner of a Classic Rover will inspect a potential purchase with a clear idea of the ills to which the model in question is prone; even better, he will seek the assistance of a fellow-enthusiast who is familiar with the model.

One thing which is worth bearing in mind from the outset, as it applies to all the 1934-1977 Rovers (certain later P6s excepted) is that their sumptuous wood-and-leather interiors can be very expensive to restore. As a poor interior destroys one of the essential Rover characteristics, it is worth double-checking that any necessary repairs really are feasible. Although wood can be revarnished, it is not easy to get a finish as good as the original, and the cost of leather repairs puts major restoration of damaged upholstery beyond the means of the average enthusiast.

Going on to consider the model ranges one by one, it is comforting to report that those cars built between 1934 and 1947 (*ie*, prior to P3) have a strong chassis, and unless there are obvious signs of severe rusting, accident damage, or the like, this component will probably be sound. Spring shackles do seize, but unless springs have broken in consequence this is not too great a problem. Mechanical brakes are frequently badly adjusted, which can account for odd braking behaviour, while those models fitted with hydraulic brakes are subject to the same problems as are found with modern hydraulic systems – corrosion of pipes, perished hoses and so on. Wire wheels should be checked for damage, if they are fitted. Pre-1937 cars had a nasty habit of breaking half-shafts, but by now most will have been fitted with the stronger replacements Rover offered after that date.

The main enemy of pre-P3 bodies (particularly Tourers) is rot in the timber framing. Reframing is expensive, time-consuming and frustrating, so a car with this sort of problem is best avoided. Chronic wood-rot can often be detected by its smell, and by a general mustiness about the car, while doors which drop when opened are a further indicator of trouble with the body frame. One good way of checking overall structural soundness is to jump (lightly) on the running-boards, although it is not a technique generally appreciated by the seller!

On the mechanical side, the best way to check if all is in order is by a road-test. The 100mm engine does rattle after high mileages as there is no timing chain tensioner to take up the slack in the chain, but this need not cause undue concern unless valve and timing troubles are suspected as well. All gearboxes will whine in first gear, but a rattle when the clutch is depressed will indicate a worn gearbox layshaft. Neglected or blocked Bijur lubrication systems will provoke all kinds of problems unless chassis greasing has been regularly carried out, and it is worth remembering that these systems are troublesome and will often have been disconnected.

The structural side of P3 models presents special problems as there is no chassis behind the rear axle and the rear springs are attached at their rearmost ends to a crossmember mounted on the body. The poor quality of much early postwar steel has ensured that rusty rear ends have sealed the fate of many otherwise serviceable cars. On suspect examples, a realistic assessment should be made of whether repairs are economically feasible; after 30 years, major surgery will almost certainly be needed if it has not already been carried out.

The front suspension of a P3 should also be examined closely. Coil springs have been unobtainable for some time and a car which needs extensive work on the IFS is probably only of scrap value. Engines are not usually problematical, although high-mileage or neglected examples do consume prodigious quantities of oil.

The P3, of course, was the first Rover fitted with the IOE engine, which in various forms powered all P4 models except the 80, as well as the six-cylinder P5s and certain variants of the Land-Rover. P3s had no oil filtration arrangements as standard, although a canister-type external filter was available as a bolt-on extra. When the P4 arrived in 1949, an oil filter became standard, but the Wipac type fitted to the early cars has not been available for many years, and it is prudent to check what, if any, alternative arrangements have been made.

P4s used three basic varieties of the IOE engine: the original P3 type was fitted in the pre-1955 75 (albeit with changed cylinder head, inlet manifold and carburation), a revised 'spread-bore' type powered the 60, 90, later 75 and all 105 models, while the third type – developed from the 3-litre engine with its seven-bearing crankshaft and revised valvegear arrangements – was fitted to 100, 95 and 110 models. Many parts of these engines were shared with contemporary Land-Rover models, and this eases spares availability to some extent. In all cases, a tapping noise from the top end will indicate wear in the cam followers (a simple replacement job); pre-1959 models had pad-type followers which wear more quickly than the later roller-follower type. This should not be confused with the lighter tapping made by maladjusted tappets, however. Oil consumption of IOE engines is quite high at the best of times, and will increase with age, mainly because the rubber O-rings in the inlet valve guides harden and allow lubricant to seep past into the combustion chambers. Blue smoke from the exhaust when the throttle is blipped will warn of this condition. The only other engine used in the P4 was the Land-Rover-derived OHV unit of the 80, which has no particular vices except a tendency to timing chain rattle and carburettor flat spots.

Also worth checking on P4 models is the front suspension. The kingpins are commonly packed with grease by owners instead of lubricated with EP 90 oil and this leads to rapid wear, detectable by steering wander, and sometimes to seizure. Repair costs are high. Rear leaf springs sag in their old age under the sheer weight of the car, but can always be retempered unless actually broken. Manual gearboxes were inherited in their essentials from the prewar models via the P3 and are subject to the same ailments as on the earlier cars. Sticking overdrive solenoids are also fairly common but not serious, and as for the automatic transmission of the 105R, that is fortunately a robust unit which does not normally give trouble.

P4s are not normally put out of commission by rust, because of their immensely strong chassis, although the outriggers which bear the body mountings can corrode badly and jacking points may also be rendered unsafe. On 1960 season and later cars, the rear chassis side-members above the axle are prone to corrosion, which may in extreme cases be compounded by stress; no-one has yet satisfactorily explained the cause of the problem because the chassis is identical to that of pre-1960 models on which this fault is very rarely found! Still underneath the car, a particular weakness is the metal box which protects the handbrake ratchet mechanism; it can corrode right away, leaving the handbrake mechanism to be attacked by road dirt, which will eventually lead to seizure or some other malfunction. Rust, of course, can make an unsightly mess of front wings; on pre-1957 cars the favourite corrosion spot is on the horizontal surface above the wheel, while on later models mud build-up causes rot to break out around the sidelights and indicators. The lower trailing edge of front wings on all P4s is also a weak spot, and rust will commonly be found in addition around the rear wheelarch (particularly the leading edge and under the body finisher trim), on the rear valances and on the spare wheel door and its hinges on post-Cyclops cars. The bottom of the B/C-post is another rust-prone area and, of course, the doors on steel-panelled cars can quickly turn into lacework once rust has taken hold.

Most of the P4's rust problems are cosmetic, but rust is very definitely the main enemy to look for when inspecting the later cars. The P5's biggest weakness is in its rear quarters, where rust will attack the D-posts and the inner members behind the wings. The early signs of this condition are rusty forward edges to the rear wings, and although a car is readily salvageable if the rust has gone no further, there are many on which new wings have been fitted over rust. New D-posts have been unobtainable for some time, so repairs will have to be made by insertion of new metal. Rust also attacks the P5's sills, and rotted inner sills will weaken the load-bearing structure to a degree which leads MOT testers to refuse a pass certificate; bent or missing jacking points are a sure sign of trouble which has not been fully rectified. Other structural problems are few, although subframe mountings can rust through and make a car unroadworthy. It is probably generally true to say that a car which looks rusty on the outer panels will be even worse underneath.

Rear springs on P5s sag just like those on P4s, and for the same reason. Front suspension ball-joints are expensive to replace if worn, and wear is detectable through steering shimmy. All PAS systems leak a little, but chronic leaks are a sign of expensive trouble. Jerky or seriously leaky automatic transmissions also herald high repair bills, the more so on pre-Mk III cars with the DG transmission, which cannot be removed from the car independently of the engine. Spares for the DG transmission are hard to find. On V8-engined cars, the type 35 transmission was near to the limit of its torque capacity and it is not uncommon for a thoughtless driver to ruin a gearbox within 50,000 miles or so.

The P5's IOE engine and manual gearbox are subject to the same problems as their P4 counterparts, but the V8 engine is a rather different matter. Its two weaknesses are its alloy construction (waterways corrode and this leads to overheating problems unless the maker's instructions with regard to the cooling system are carried out) and its valvegear. Early examples wore rocker shafts very quickly, although by now most will have been rebuilt with the improved type, and sooner or later the valving of the hydraulic tappets inevitably clogs with oil sludge, leading to noisy valvegear. As the tappets are, of course, non-adjustable, they must be replaced, at some expense, although the type introduced in 1976 for the SD1 models can be used and are said to have a longer life. Another common fault is the light knocking caused by camshaft wear, but this can usually be disregarded. All V8 engines in P5B cars were designed to run on 5-star (100-octane) petrol, which ceased to be available in the late 1970s. Owners have a choice of rebuilding with low-compression pistons (rare), retarding the ignition timing (a compromise), or doing nothing at all (all too common). In the latter case, misfiring will be apparent under load, and even with retarded ignition the engines may consume exhaust valves in short order.

As the P6B's engine and (automatic) gearbox were the same as the P5B's until 1973, the same comments apply. The type 65 automatic gearbox used after that date is rather more durable than its predecessor, but again leaks may warn of trouble; and the lower-compression engines have exactly the same valvegear and corrosion problems as their early counterparts, even though they are happy on 4-star fuel. The OHC engines of the 2000 and 2200 are long-lived units, although timing chain rattle is very common and indicates a need for adjustment, while tuning of the twin-carburettor models in not as easy as it might appear and is in consequence commonly neglected. Oil leaks from the cam covers of the four-cylinder engines are quite common, but are not worrying unless serious. All 2000TC models required 5-star petrol like the pre-1974 season V8s, and unless they have been detuned are likely to burn exhaust valves and to misfire.

Early P6 manual gearboxes are rather notchy and often difficult to put into gear. Noise in neutral indicates worn layshaft bearings, which are more common on pre-1969 season cars. Pre-1972 season gear levers may feel sloppy, but this is to be expected and need not cause concern. On 3500S models it is advisable to look out for a gearbox which has been thrashed by an over-enthusiastic owner. Slipping clutches on all models indicate expensive work ahead, as the engine must be removed before a replacement unit is fitted on a 2000/2200 and the gearbox must come out on a 3500S. (It is just possible to do the job *in situ* on a 2000/2200SC, but certainly not on a TC car.) Driveline clonks in all models are common and are often caused by worn universal joints, of which there are two per driveshaft. Early differentials will often leak oil over the rear brake discs and, also at the rear, the De Dion sliding tube is protected by a rubber gaiter which can split and allow road filth to build up and hinder the correct functioning of the sliding joint.

Although it is normal for P6 steering to be on the heavy side, excessively stiff steering may indicate that lubrication of the steering box and idler has been neglected. Power steering systems, of course, leak in exactly the same way as those on P5s. The P6s are especially sensitive to correct wheel alignment and balance and can wear front tyres very quickly; power-steered cars are the worst offenders in this respect. Brakes are not normally troublesome, although the early Dunlop type were prone to sticking pistons, which in extreme cases could lead to broken discs. P6 springs and dampers are relatively soft for a car with such handling/performance potential and such softness need not be an indication of suspension trouble.

The very worst trap to fall into when buying a P6, however, is to go for a car which has had new outer panels put on over a rusty base-unit. At the time of writing, outer panels are still in plentiful supply, and rusty ones are commonly replaced to disguise more serious problems underneath. Rust usually starts at the rear edge of the front wings and the leading edge of the rear wings, and then works inwards. Sills also corrode and their inner surfaces should always be checked (the outer sills are bolt-on panels with no structural function); warning of corrosion may first be seen inside the car underneath the kick-plates. The boot floor will often rot through and render the boot useless, although this is not a structural problem except in the very worst cases. If in doubt about corrosion in a potential P6 purchase it is always wiser to err on the side of safety; it cannot be stressed enough that a P6 rusts even more seriously than a P5 (particularly the earlier cars with their less effective underbody protection), and that a badly-corroded base-unit is so expensive to repair that a car with severe problems here is probably best regarded as a complete write-off.

CHAPTER 9

Maintaining a Classic Rover

Spares, services and the clubs

Perhaps the first thing to recognize about the spares and maintenance situation for Classic Rovers is that although the Rover name survives, the parent company no longer exists, but is split between the Austin Rover Group, British Leyland's volume car division, and Land-Rover Limited, who build the four-wheel-drive vehicles. Add to that the fact that spare parts are handled by another Leyland division known as Unipart, and it is easy to see that factory support is at best diversified, and at worst can be non-existent. As Unipart explained to the author, they try to keep Rover mechanical parts in stock for 10 years after a model has ceased production, and body or trim parts for five years, but for good business reasons they have to make compromises. Stocks of slow-moving spares take up valuable storage space, and British Leyland is not yet so overburdened with profits that it can afford such storage, let alone to remanufacture obsolete out-of-stock items. Thus, if it is possible to fit a choke cable, for example, from a later model or even a totally different car, then this is what Unipart will supply when stocks of the original item are exhausted. Similar good business reasons mean that no Rover agent will worry about not having a mechanic who is familiar with the pre-P6 cars when he cannot expect more than one or two vehicles of that age through his workshops in any given month.

So the Classic Rover owner has to come to terms with two facts of life: the non-availability through normal retail outlets of many or most of the spare parts he wants, and the rapidly dwindling number of mechanics who have enough experience of the cars to carry out competent servicing and maintenance work. At the time of writing, Unipart are already deleting non-essential spares for the early P6 cars from their lists (ie, those not necessary to keep a car in running order), although P6 servicing expertise is still readily available from most Austin Rover agents. Inevitably, though, this situation will deteriorate – so how can the Classic Rover owner expect to keep his car in the sort of condition of which he can be proud?

Fortunately, all is far from lost, although it should be noted that Rovers are not as well catered for by the classic car and other aftermarket specialists as are, for example, Jaguars and MGs, even though the recent rise to popularity of the P4 range has led to a significant increase in the number of specialists who cater for these models. Owners of pre-P4 Rovers should remember that their cars do not have the kind of international following which would make it worth anyone's while setting up in business to deal solely with their care and restoration. Of course, pre-P4 specialists do exist, but they tend to be enthusiasts who work on the cars or supply spares and remanufactured parts in their free time. As it would be unfair to them and to their families to publish names and addresses here (they have other things to do with their lives as well as talk Rovers to all and sundry), pre-P4 enthusiasts are advised to contact them through the owners' clubs – of which more in a moment.

Nevertheless, a number of enthusiasts do offer a professional service to owners of cars of all ages. Longest-established of these Rover specialists is Richard Stenning, of Masquerade, 22-24 Silver Street, Wiveliscombe, Taunton,

Somerset (telephone 0984-23641), who will work on or supply parts for all the 1933-1977 cars, while Geoff Kent, of 11 Woodland Gardens, London N10 3UE, aims to stock all spares, as well as sales, workshop and owners' literature, for the cars. It is best to telephone him first on 01-883-1800, mornings or evenings, but overseas customers may prefer to write. Parts for the P4 range, including certain remanufactured items, can also be obtained from P4 Spares at 60 Woodville Road, London NW11 9TN, but again a preliminary phone call should be made, on 01-455-6992, any day except Saturday. Still in London, P4, P5 and (especially) P6 spares are held by Chris Wickham, who can be contacted in the evenings on 01-660-6722; and suppliers in the north are John Mann, of Chesterfield (telephone 0246-71036), and Keith Oxley, at 40B Hammersmith, Ripley, Derbyshire DE5 3RA (0773-46048). The former supplies spares for P3 and later cars, while the latter is a P5 spares specialist.

In addition to these individuals, a number of specialist firms cater for Rover owners. Best known for their P4 work, the BL Heritage-approved Rover people in the London and Home Counties area are DAK Autos Ltd, of Unit 3B, Lye Trading Estate, Old Bedford Road, Luton, Bedfordshire (0582-416789). In the Midlands, rebuilds of P4 and earlier cars are undertaken by RHW of Coventry, who have also remanufactured a number of body panels and designed repair sections for all these models. They can be found at The Arches Industrial Estate, Spon End, Coventry, (telephone 0203-713026). Many spares for P5 and P6 models can be obtained from J & R Spares, Castle Road, Clacton-on-Sea, Essex (telephone 0255-28649/25428, while Herongate Motor Company, of Park Farm, Dunton Road, Herongate, Brentwood, Essex (0227-810098) keep stocks of new and secondhand parts for P4 and later models, and can also undertake work on these cars. The P6 specialists, for both parts and mechanical or body work, are the Rover Centre, 318 Lea Bridge Road, London E10 7LD (telephone 01-556-5442 or 01-558-2975); and stocks of spares for pre-1966 Rovers are kept by Roverpart of Lewisham, 108 Cudham Lane North, Cudham, Sevenoaks, Kent.

Finally, on the subject of spares, glass-fibre wings for P4, P5 and P6 models have been available for some time through a number of retailers (see *Exchange and Mart* or the classic car press for details), and P5 outer sill panels in metal are also available through some replacement panel specialists – although a word of caution is necessary here because some varieties available are incorrectly contoured and lack the turned-over end-pieces of the Rover-made panels.

Many Classic Rover owners will wish to carry out their own maintenance and restoration work as far as possible, and the very minimum requirement for this is possession of the Owner's Instruction Manual with which all cars were delivered (later vehicles also came with an Owner's Maintenance Manual). For any restoration or major maintenance work, a Parts Book and a Workshop Manual are also indispensable. In the latter case, the official Rover item is infinitely preferable to the variety of cheaper manuals on P4, P5 and P6 which have been available over the years.

Just as stocks of spares held by Austin Rover are allowed to run low, so stocks of handbooks, Parts Books, and Workshop Manuals are not replenished once a vehicle is long out of production. Although specialist bookshops and autojumbles may often be able to provide copies of the relevant literature, the best solution is often to go through the owners' clubs, where a fellow-enthusiast can usually help with the loan of material, even if it is impossible to secure a copy of a particular item. P4 owners are particularly fortunate in that both the Workshop Manual and the Parts Books have been reprinted by the Rover P4 Drivers' Guild, while the relevant Service Newsletters have been reprinted by the Rover Sports Register. P6 literature is still mostly available from Unipart at the time of writing, but P5 owners will have to search a little harder in most cases. P3 owners will experience difficulty in finding literature because so few of the cars were built that relatively small quantities of the literature were produced. Cars prior to the P3 were never covered by an official Workshop Manual, although from time to time Rover did issue Service Newsletters, mainly devoted to changes in specification. The Rover Sports Register has made a major contribution to the maintenance of these older vehicles by republishing the official Parts Books, and issuing a Workshop Manual compiled by experts within the club. The latter is a long-term undertaking and is being published in stages; it caters for all models built between 1933 and 1947.

Of course, the clubs offer a great deal more value to the enthusiast than as sources of rare literature, and Rover enthusiasts are strongly recommended to join, if only to feel secure in the knowledge that there are others who share the same time-consuming, money-consuming passion! Contact addresses are given below, but club officers do change from time to time, so these addresses should be checked against details available in the classic car press before a letter is written. As the clubs exist on members' subscriptions, and are run by volunteers, letters not accompanied by an SAE are most unlikely to receive an answer.

There are two major clubs in Britain. These are the Rover Sports Register, which was founded in 1953 to cater for owners of Rover Sports Tourers, but now welcomes all Rover owners; and the Rover P4 Drivers' Guild, founded in 1977 specifically for owners of the P4 models. Membership of each club is around 1,500 at the time of writing – which testifies to the present popularity of the P4 models – but the two clubs are in no sense rivals; inevitably, they have many members in common and they arrange a number of joint events. Contact addresses are as follows:

Rover Sports Register	Cliff Evans
	87 Herbert Jennings Avenue
	Wexham
	Clwyd
	LL12 7YA
Rover P4 Drivers' Guild	Colin Blowers
	32 Arundel Road
	Luton
	Bedfordshire
	LU4 8DY

Both clubs are affiliated to the Association of Rover Clubs, an umbrella organization uniting the car and Land-Rover clubs, which provides a link with the remains of the parent company. The RSR and P4 Guild both organize regional meetings throughout the year, and larger regional and national events during the summer months. These latter almost invariably include a *Concours d'élégance* for those whose interest lies in that direction. The RSR also organize an annual driving test competition and a weekend rally in the Lake District. Both clubs produce a bi-monthly magazine, *Freewheel* in the case of the RSR, and *Overdrive* for the P4 Guild, together with Newsletters in the intervening months. These publications carry the fundamental necessities of all club magazines – event dates and For Sale and Wanted advertisements – as well as useful technical articles and interesting historical material. The P4 Guild also produces a Yearbook for its members, with an invaluable list of recommended firms and suppliers.

Technical advice is freely available from appointed experts in both clubs; the RSR has Librarians, who can usually provide photocopies of published technical information or other literature; and the P4 Guild runs a splendid network of National Breakdown Volunteers, who can assist members in trouble. From time to time, individuals in both clubs organize the manufacture of batches of reproduction parts; recent efforts within the RSR, for example, have included a number of rubber bushes for the earlier cars. Other members offer reconditioning services for such items as dynamos, starters, brake calipers and servos, and even body panels.

1982 saw the foundation of two new clubs, which is doubtless an indication of the growing appreciation of Rovers generally as classic cars. The Rover 3/3½-litre Club has as its main aim to keep these models on the road, and potential members should write to Dr J.P. Dickenson, at 21 Hyde Park Corner, Leeds 6. P6 enthusiasts are also now served by their own club, and the P6 Rover Owners' Club can be contacted through its Treasurer, Dr M.J. Beetham, at 11 Coleshill Place, Bradwell Common, Milton Keynes MK13 8DG. Several regional clubs also exist in the UK, such as the Southern Rover Owners' Club, the Norfolk and Norwich P4 Owners' Club and the Torquay and Torbay Rover Owners' Club, and there are several overseas clubs which have links with their British counterparts. These include the Rover Owners' Club (Holland), the Rover

Owners' Association of Queensland (Australia), and the Rover Owners' Club of New Zealand.

For those interested in historical information, several books exist, and it is worth checking that any information required has not already been published before turning to the very helpful but overburdened staff of BL Heritage, at Studley Castle, Manor Road, Studley, Warwickshire. Regrettably, both *Rover Memories: an illustrated survey of the Rover car* by Richard Hough and Michael Frostick (Allen and Unwin, 1966), and *The Rover* by George Oliver (Cassell, 1971), are out of print, but copies can occasionally be found. A very readable general history of the Rover Company and its products is given in Graham Robson's *The Rover Story* (Patrick Stephens, 1976; second, revised edition, 1981), while the detailed history of two models is contained in the present author's *The Postwar Rover: P4 and P5* (P4 Spares, 1981). In addition, Brooklands Books have published three volumes of road-test reprints, *Rover P4, 1949-1959, Rover P4, 1955-1964 and Rover 3 & 3.5-litre, 1958-1973,* all of which are readily available

APPENDIX A
Technical specifications

(Note: unless otherwise specified, all dates refer to model-year).

1934-40 and 1946-47 models

10hp, produced 1934-40, 1946-47

Construction: Separate chassis and ash-framed body with steel panels.
Engine: 4-cyl, 66.5mm x 100mm, 1,389cc OHV. RAC rating 10.9hp. 5.9:1 CR (1934-38); 6.25:1 CR (1939-47). 3-bearing crankshaft, single SU carburettor. 44bhp SAE at 4,200rpm (1934-38); 48bhp approx (1939-47). Twin-carburettor engine optionally available (1938-40).
Transmission: 4-speed gearbox with reverse and freewheel; 1939-47 models have synchromesh on 3rd and 4th gears. Gear ratios 4.05:1, 2.25:1, 1.52:1, 1:1, (1934-38); 3.5:1, 2.25:1, 1.5:1, 1:1, (1939); 3.37:1, 2.03:1, 1.48:1, 1:1, (1940); 3.37:1, 2.04:1, 1.49:1, 1:1, (1946-47). Axle ratio 4.88:1. Top gear 16.4mph/1,000rpm (1940-47).
Steering, suspension and brakes: Semi-elliptic leaf springs front and rear with hydraulic piston-type shock absorbers. Marles Weller cam-and-roller steering (1934); Burman Douglas worm-and-nut steering (1935-47). Harmonic stabilizer in front bumper. Girling mechanical brakes with 12in drums. 4.50 x 18 tyres on wire wheels (1934-36); 4.75 x 18 (1937-38); 4.75 x 17 tyres on 17in wheels (1939-47); pressed-steel disc wheels optional 1939, standard 1940-47. 1934 export models have 4.75 x 20 tyres on 20in wheels.
Dimensions: Wheelbase 105in (1934-39); 105.5in (1940-47). Front track 50in. Rear track 51.5in. Length 152in (Saloon). Width 61in (1934-39 Saloon); 62in (1940-47 Saloon). Height 62.5in (1946-47 Saloon). Ground clearance 6.5in (1934-36); 6.25in (1937-47). Dry weight 2,688lb approx (1934-38 Saloon and Sports Saloon); 2,800lb approx (1939-47 Saloon and Sports Saloon); 2,688lb approx (Coupe). Turning circle 37ft.
Body styles available: 6-light Saloon; 4-light Sports Saloon (1934, 1937-47); Coupe (1934, 1938-40); Tourer (1934); Chassis available separately for custom-built coachwork (1934-37).

12hp, produced 1934-40, 1946-47

As 10hp except:
Engine: 4-cyl, 69mm x 100mm, 1,496cc OHV. RAC rating 11.9hp. 5.7:1 CR (1934-38); 6.25:1 CR (1939-47). 3-bearing crankshaft, single SU carburettor. 48bhp SAE at 4,200rpm (1934-38); 53bhp approx (1939-47). Twin-carburettor, high-compression engine optionally available 1936-1940.
Transmission: Top gear 16.6mph/1,000rpm (1940-47).
Steering, suspension and brakes: Front and rear anti-roll bars (1940-47). 4.75 x 18 tyres (1934-36); 5.00 x 18 (1937); 5.25 x 17 (1938-47). 1934 export models have 4.75 x 20 tyres on 20in wheels.
Dimensions: Wheelbase 105in (1934-36); 112in (1937-47, and all 6-light Saloons 1935-47). Front track 50in, Rear track 51.5in (1934-39); 54in (1940-47). Length 156in (1934-36 Sports Saloon); 160in (1935-36 Saloon); 161in (1934-36 Tourer); 169.5in (1937-47). Width 62in (1937-47). Height 63in (1934-47 Saloon); 61in (1937-47 Sports Saloon). Ground clearance 6.5in; 5.5in (1934-36 Sports Saloon). Dry weight 2,688lb approx (1934-36 Saloon and Sports Saloon);

2,912lb approx (1937-47 Saloon and Sports Saloon). Turning circle 39ft.
Body styles available: 6-light Saloon; 4-light Sports Saloon; Coupe (1934); Tourer (1934-36, 1947). Chassis available separately for custom-built coachwork, (1934-37).

14hp, produced 1934-40, 1946-47, and Speed 14, produced 1934-36.

As 12hp, except:
Engine: (1934-38) 6-cyl, 61mm x 90mm, 1,577cc OHV. RAC rating 13.9hp. 6.1:1 CR; 6.7:1 (Speed 14). 4-bearing crankshaft, single SU carburettor; triple downdraught SU carburettors (Speed 14). 48bhp SAE at 4,600rpm; 54bhp at 4,800rpm (Speed 14). Speed 14 engine optionally available on 14hp, 1936. (1939-47) 6-cyl, 63.5mm x 100mm, 1,901cc OHV. RAC rating 14.9hp. 6.25:1 CR (1939); 6.5:1 CR (1940-47). 4-bearing crankshaft, single SU carburettor (1939); Solex dual downdraught carburettor (1940-47); triple-carburettor engine optionally available 1939-40. Power outputs never quoted.
Transmission: Axle ratio 5.22:1; 4.88:1 (Speed 14 and all models with triple-carburettor engine). Top gear 17.1mph/1,000rpm (1940-47).
Steering, suspension and brakes: Front and rear anti-roll bars (1939-47). Lockheed hydraulic brakes with 12in drums (1934-35); Girling mechanical brakes with 12in drums (1936-47). 4.75 x 18 tyres (1934); 5.25 x 17 (1935-38); 5.50 x 17 (1939-47); 5.00 x 18 (Speed 14). 1934 export models have 4.75 x 20 tyres on 20in wheels.
Dimensions: Wheelbase 115in. Front track 50in (1934--38); 52in (1939-47). Rear track 51.5in (1934-39); 54in (1940-47). Length 165in (1934-36 Saloon); 172.5in (1937-47). Width 61in (1934-36); 62in (1937-47). Height 64in (1937-47 Saloon); 61in (1937-47 Sports Saloon). Ground clearance 6.75in (1934-36); 6.5in (1937-47). Dry weight 2,912lb approx (1934-36 Saloon and Sports Saloon); 3,136lb approx (1937-38); 3,192lb approx (1939-47); 3,304lb approx (Drophead Coupe). Turning circle 40ft.
Body styles available: 14hp – 6-light Saloon; 4-light Sports Saloon; Coupe (1934); Tourer (1934); Streamline Saloon (1935-36); Streamline Coupe (1935-36); Drophead Coupe (1939-40). Chassis available separately for custom-built coachwork (1934-37). Speed 14 – Sports Saloon; Tourer; Hastings Coupe (1934); Streamline Coupe (1935-36). Chassis available separately for custom-built coachwork.

16hp, produced 1937-40, 1946-47

As contemporary 14hp, except:
Engine: 6-cyl, 67.5mm x 100mm, 2,147cc OHV. RAC rating 16.9hp. 5.9:1 CR (1937); 6.1:1 CR (1938-39); 6.5:1 CR (1940-47). 4-bearing crankshaft, single SU carburettor (1937-39); Solex dual downdraught carburettor (1940-47); triple-carburettor engine optionally available (1939-40). 60bhp SAE at 4,600rpm (1937-39); 66bhp approx (1940-47). Power output of triple-carburettor engine never quoted.
Transmission: Axle ratio 4.7:1. Top gear 17.7mph/1,000rpm (1940-47).
Steering, suspension and brakes: 5.50 x 17 tyres.

20hp, produced 1937-40 (known as 'Speed 20', 1937).
As contemporary 16hp, except:
Engine: 6-cyl, 73mm x 100mm, 2,512cc OHV. RAC rating 19.8hp. 6.1:1 CR (1937-39); 6.5:1 CR (1940). 4-bearing crankshaft, single SU carburettor (1937-39); Solex dual downdraught carburettor (1940). Power output never quoted.
Transmission: Axle ratio 4.5:1 Top gear 18.5mph/1,000rpm.
Body styles available: Sports Saloon; Drophead Coupe (1939-40).
Chassis available separately for custom-built coachwork (1937).

P3 models

60, produced 1948-49
Construction: Separate three-quarter chassis and all-steel body.
Engine: 4-cyl, 69.5mm x 105mm, 1,595cc IOE. 7.1:1 CR. 3-bearing crankshaft, single Solex downdraught carburettor. 60bhp SAE.
Transmission: 4-speed gearbox with reverse and freewheel; synchromesh on 3rd and 4th gears. Gear ratios 3.37:1, 2.04:1, 1.48:1, 1:1, reverse 2.97:1. Axle ratio 4.7:1. Top gear 17.1mph/1,000rpm (with 17in wheels); 16.7mph/1,000rpm (with 16in wheels).
Steering, suspension and brakes: Independent front suspension with coil springs and anti-roll torsion bar; semi-elliptic rear springs; hydraulic shock absorbers, piston-type at the front and telescopic-type at the rear (telescopic front shock absorbers fitted for 1949). Burman Douglas recirculating-ball steering. Girling hydro-mechanical brakes with 12in drums. 5.25 x 17 tyres on pressed-steel disc wheels (5.75 tyres on 16in wheels optional).
Dimensions: Wheelbase 110.5in. Front track 51.187in. Rear track 54.875in. Length 171.25in. Width 63in. Height 65in (6-light bodies); 62in (4-light bodies). Ground clearance 7.625in. Dry weight 2,968lb approx (6-light bodies); 2,940lb approx (4-light bodies). Turning circle 37ft.

75, produced 1948-49
As 60, except:
Engine: 6-cyl, 65.2mm x 105mm, 2,103cc IOE. 7.25:1 CR. 4-bearing crankshaft, Solex dual downdraught carburettor. 72bhp SAE at 4,000rpm.
Transmission: Top gear 17.35mph/1,000rpm (with 17in wheels); 16.7mph/1,000rpm (with optional 16in wheels).
Steering, suspension and brakes: 5.50 x 17 tyres (5.75 tyres on 16in wheels optional).
Dimensions: Ground clearance 7.875in. Dry weight 3,108lb approx (6-light bodies); 3,080lb approx (4-light bodies).

P4 models

60, produced 1954-59
Construction: Separate chassis and all-steel body with aluminium doors, bonnet and bootlid.
Engine: 4-cyl, 77.8mm x 105mm, 1,997cc IOE. 6.73:1 CR (1954-56); 6.92:1 CR (1957-59). 3-bearing crankshaft, single SU carburettor. 60bhp SAE at 4,000rpm. Max torque 101lb/ft SAE at 2,000rpm.
Transmission: 4-speed gearbox with reverse and freewheel (overdrive optional instead of freewheel (1957-59); synchromesh on 2nd, 3rd and 4th gears. Gear ratios 3.37:1, 2.04:1, 1.37:1, 1:1, reverse 2.97:1, overdrive 0.77:1. Axle ratio 4.3:1 (4.7:1 with overdrive). Top gear 18mph/1,000rpm; overdrive 21.2mph/1,000rpm.
Steering, suspension and brakes: Independent front suspension with coil springs and anti-roll torsion bar; semi-floating rear axle with constant-rate semi-elliptic springs; hydraulic telescopic shock absorbers. Burman recirculating-ball, worm-and-nut steering with variable ratio. Hydraulic brakes with 11in drums. 6.00 x 15 tyres on pressed steel disc wheels with 4.5in rims (6.40 x 15 tyres optional 1959).
Dimensions: Wheelbase 111in. Front track 52in. Rear track 51.5in. Length 178.25in. (178.625in, 1959). Width 65.625in. Height 63.75in. Ground clearance 7.125in. Running weight 3,106lb (3,148lb with overdrive). Turning circle 37ft.
Body styles available: Saloon.

75, produced 1950-59
As 60, except:
Engine: (1950-54) 6-cyl, 65.2mm x 105mm, 2,103cc IOE. 7.25:1 CR. 4-bearing crankshaft, twin SU carburettors. 75bhp SAE at 4,200rpm. Max torque 111lb/ft SAE at 2,500rpm. (1955-59) 6-cyl, 73.025mm x 88.9mm, 2,230cc IOE. 6.95:1 CR (1955-56); 7.2:1 CR (1957-59). 4-bearing crankshaft, single SU carburettor. 80bhp SAE at 4,500rpm. Max torque 113lb/ft SAE at 1,750rpm.
Transmission: 1950-53 models have no synchromesh on 2nd gear.
Steering, suspension and brakes: Progressive-rate semi-elliptic rear springs. 1950-52 models have Panhard rod attached to rear axle casing. 1950 models have mechanically-operated rear brakes.
Dimensions: Running weight 3,265lb (1950-54); 3,262lb (1955-59); 3,304lb (with overdrive).

80, produced 1960-62
As 75, except:
Engine: 4-cyl, 90.47mm x 88.8mm, 2,286cc OHV. 7:1 CR. 3-bearing crankshaft, single Solex carburettor. 77bhp SAE at 4,250rpm. Max torque 124lb/ft SAE at 2,500rpm.
Transmission: Overdrive gearbox standard; some non-overdrive cars built, 1960. Axle ratio 4.3:1 (with or without overdrive). Top gear 17.8mph/1,000rpm; overdrive 22.8mph/1,000rpm.
Steering, suspension and brakes: Servo-assisted hydraulic brakes with 10.7in diameter discs at front, 11in drums at rear. 6.40 x 15 tyres optional.
Dimensions: Front track 52.5in. Length 178.625in. Running weight 3,204lb (3,246lb with overdrive).

90, produced 1954-59
As 75, except:
Engine: 6-cyl, 73.025mm x 105mm, 2,638cc IOE. 6.25:1 CR (1954); 6.73:1 CR (1955); 7.5:1 CR (1956-59). 4-bearing crankshaft, single SU carburettor. 90bhp SAE at 4,500rpm (1954-55); 93bhp at 4,500rpm (1956-59). Max torque 130lb/ft SAE at 1,500rpm (1954-55); 138lb/ft at 1,750rpm (1956-59).
Transmission: Overdrive optional (1956-59); freewheel available (1954-55). Axle ratio 4.3:1 (with or without overdrive); 3.9:1 optional (1955) with freewheel only. Top gear (4.3 axle) 18mph/1,000rpm; overdrive 23.3mph/1,000rpm.
Steering, suspension and brakes: Servo-assisted hydraulic brakes with 11in drums available with optional overdrive only (1955-59).
Dimensions: Running weight 3,200lb (1954-55); 3,245lb (1956-57); 3,276lb (1956-57, with overdrive); 3,267lb (1958-59); 3,309lb (1958-59, with overdrive).

95, produced 1963-64
As 80 except:
Construction: Cars built after March 1963 have all-steel panels.
Engine: 6-cyl, 77.8mm x 92.075mm, 2,625cc IOE. 8.8:1 CR (7.8:1 CR optional). 7-bearing crankshaft, single SU carburettor. 102bhp SAE at 4,750rpm (100bhp at 4,750rpm, low-compression models). Max torque 140lb/ft SAE at 1,500rpm

(136lb/ft at 1,500rpm, low-compression models).
Transmission: 4-speed and reverse gearbox without freewheel or overdrive.
Axle ratio 3.9:1. Top gear 19mph/1,000rpm.
Dimensions: Running weight 3,287lb.

100, produced 1960-62
As 95, except:
Engine: 7.8:1 CR. 104bhp SAE at 4,750rpm. Max torque 138lb/ft SAE at 1,500rpm.
Transmission: Overdrive gearbox standard; some non-overdrive cars built (1960). Axle ratio 4.3:1 (with or without overdrive). Top gear 17.8mph/1,000rpm; overdrive 22.8mph/1,000rpm.
Dimensions: Running weight 3,267lb (3,309lb with overdrive).

105R, produced 1957-58
As 90, except:
Engine: 8.5:1 CR (7.5:1 optional). Twin SU carburettors. 108bhp SAE at 4,250rpm. Max torque 152lb/ft SAE at 2,500rpm.
Transmission: Roverdrive automatic transmission, consisting of torque convertor, 2-speed synchromesh gearbox with reverse, and automatic overdrive. Gear ratios 1.74:1, 1:1, reverse 2.9:1, overdrive 0.77:1; torque convertor ratio variable between 2.18:1 and 1:1. Axle ratio 4.7:1. Top gear 21.2mph/1000rpm (= overdrive).
Steering, suspension and brakes: Servo-assisted hydraulic brakes with 11in drums.

105S, produced 1957-58, and 105, produced 1959
As 105R, except:
Transmission: Overdrive gearbox standard; ratios and synchromesh as for 60. Top gear 18mph/1,000rpm; overdrive 23.3mph/1,000rpm.
Steering, suspension and brakes: 6.40 x 15 tyres optional on 105 only.
Dimensions: Length 178.625in (105 only). Running weight 3,382lb (105S); 3,284lb (105).

110, produced 1963-64
As 100, except:
Construction: Cars built after March 1963 have all-steel panels.
Engine: 8.8:1 CR (7.8:1 CR optional). 123bhp SAE at 5,000rpm (121bhp at 5,000rpm, low-compression models). Max torque 142lb/ft SAE at 3,000rpm (136lb/ft at 3,000rpm, low-compression models).
Transmission: All cars fitted with overdrive. Top gear 17.5mph/1,000rpm; overdrive 22.7mph/1,000rpm.
Dimensions: Running weight 3,354lb.

P5 and P5B models

3-litre Mk I, produced 1959-61
Construction: All-steel monocoque with separate front subframe.
Engine: 6-cyl, 77.8mm x 105mm, 2,995cc IOE. 8.75:1 CR (7.5:1 optional on export models). 7-bearing crankshaft, single SU carburettor. 115bhp SAE at 4,500rpm. Max torque 164lb/ft SAE at 1,500rpm.
Transmission: 4-speed gearbox with reverse and optional overdrive; synchromesh on 2nd, 3rd and 4th gears. Optional Borg-Warner type DG 3-speed automatic transmission. Gear ratios (manual transmission) 3.37:1, 2.04:1, 1.37:1, 1:1, reverse 2.96:1, overdrive 0.77:1; (Automatic) 2.30:1, 1.43:1, 1:1, reverse 2.0:1. Overdrive standardized with manual transmission on 1961 models. Axle ratio 3.9:1 (4-speed and Automatic models), 4.3:1 (overdrive

model). Top gear 20.1mph/1,000rpm (3.9 axle), 18.3mph/1,000rpm (4.3 axle); overdrive 23.5mph/1,000rpm.
Steering, suspension and brakes: Independent front suspension with laminated torsion bars and anti-roll bar; semi-floating rear axle with progressive-rate semi-elliptic springs; hydraulic telescopic shock absorbers. Burman recirculating-ball variable-ratio steering; Hydrasteer variable-ratio power-assisted steering optional (1961). Servo-assisted hydraulic brakes with 11in drums, 2 trailing shoes at the front; 10.75in discs at the front (1961). 6.70 x 15 tyres (7.10 x 15 optional) on pressed-steel disc wheels with 5in rims.
Dimensions: Wheelbase 110.5in. Front track 55in. Rear track 56in. Length 186.5in. Width 70in. Height 60.25in. Ground clearance 7.875in. Running weight 3,556lb (4-speed); 3,612lb (overdrive); 3,640lb (Automatic).
Body styles available: Saloon.

3-litre Mk IA, produced 1962
As Mk I models, except:
Steering, suspension and brakes: 7.10 x 15 tyres no longer offered.

3-litre Mk II, produced 1963-66
As Mk IA models, except:
Engine: 8.75:1 CR (overdrive models); 8.0:1 (Automatic). 134bhp SAE at 5,000rpm (overdrive); 129bhp at 4,750rpm (Automatic). Max torque 169lb/ft SAE at 1,750rpm; 161lb/ft at 3,000rpm (Automatic).
Transmission: Gear ratios (overdrive models) 3.37:1, 1.88:1, 1.27:1, 1:1, reverse 2.96:1, overdrive 0.77:1. Top gear 18.68mph/1,000rpm (overdrive models); overdrive 23.8mph/1,000rpm; 20.6mph/1,000rpm (Automatic).
Suspension, steering and brakes: Power-assisted steering standard on Coupe models; standardized on Saloons (1965-66).
Dimensions: Height 59.25in (Saloon); 56.75in (Coupe). Ground clearance 6.625in. Running weight 3,640lb (Saloon, overdrive); 3,654lb (Saloon, Automatic); 3,727lb (Coupe, overdrive); 3,741lb (Coupe, Automatic).
Body styles available: Saloon, Coupe.

3-litre Mk III, produced 1966-67
As Mk II models, except:
Engine: Both overdrive and Automatic models now have 8.75:1 CR and develop 134bhp SAE at 5,000rpm, 169lb/ft of torque at 1,750rpm.
Transmission: Optional Automatic transmission now Borg-Warner type 35 3-speed. Gear ratios (Automatic models) 2.39:1, 1.45:1, 1:1, reverse 2.09:1. Axle ratio (Automatic models) 3.54:1.
Dimensions: Running weight 3,738lb (Saloon, overdrive); 3,693lb (Saloon, Automatic); 3,738lb (Coupe, overdrive); 3.702lb (Coupe, Automatic).

3.5-litre, produced 1968, and 3½-litre, produced 1969-73
As Mk III 3-litre models, except:
Engine: V8-cyl, 88.9mm x 71.1mm, 3,528cc OHV. 10.5:1 CR. 5-bearing crankshaft, twin SU carburettors. 184bhp SAE· at 5,200rpm. Max torque 226lb/ft SAE at 3,000rpm.
Transmission: Automatic only available (Borg-Warner type 35 3-speed). Gear ratios 2.39:1, 1.45:1, 1:1, reverse 2.09:1. Axle ratio 3.54:1. Top gear 21.4mph/1,000rpm.
Steering, suspension and brakes: Chromium plated and painted pressed-steel Rostyle wheels with 5in rims.
Dimensions: Front track 55.312in. Height 60in (Saloon); 58in (Coupe). Running weight 3,498lb (Saloon); 3,479lb (Coupe).

2.4-litre, produced 1962 (export only)
As contemporary 3-litre models, except:
Engine: 6-cyl, 77.8mm x 85.7mm, 2,445cc IOE.
No further details available.

2.6-litre, produced 1962-65 (export only)
As contemporary 3-litre models, except:
Engine: 6-cyl, 77.8mm x 92.075mm, 2,625cc IOE. No further details known, but probably generally similar to P4 110 engine. Transmission: Gear ratios 3.37:1, 2.04:1, 1.37:1, 1:1, reverse 2.96:1.
Body styles available: Saloon.
No further details available.

P6 and P6B models
Note: These specifications are for home market models only.

2000, produced 1964-66, and 2000SC, produced 1967-73
Construction: All-steel base-unit with outer panels and running gear bolted in place. Panels in steel except for aluminium bonnet and bootlid.
Engine: 4-cyl, 85.7mm x 85.7mm, 1,978cc OHC. 9:1 CR. 5-bearing crankshaft, single SU carburettor. 99bhp SAE at 5,000rpm; 89bhp DIN at 5,000rpm. Max torque 121lb/ft SAE at 3,600rpm; 108lb/ft DIN at 2,500rpm.
Transmission: 4-speed all-synchromesh gearbox with reverse. Gear ratios 3.62:1, 2.13:1, 1.39:1, 1:1, reverse 3.43:1. Axle ratio 3.54:1. Top gear 19.5mph/1,000rpm.
Steering, suspension and brakes: Independent front suspension by transverse bottom links and leading upper links acting on coil springs mounted horizontally to the bulkhead; anti-roll bar. Rear suspension by De Dion-type tube incorporating sliding joint, with transverse location by fixed-length drive-shafts and stabilizer rod. Fore-and-aft location by Watt linkages, with coil springs between front links and base-unit. Hydraulic telescopic shock absorbers. Adamant Marles worm-and-roller steering. Servo-assisted Dunlop disc brakes, inboard at rear, with 10.75in discs at front, 10.25in at rear (1964 – May 1966 approx); Girling units with 10.31in front discs and 10.69in rear discs (May 1966 approx – 1973). 165 SR-14 radial-ply tyres on pressed-steel disc wheels with 5in rims.
Dimensions: Wheelbase 103.375in. Front track 53.375in. Rear track 52.5in. Length 178.5in. Width 66in. Height 54.75in. Ground clearance 6.625in. Running weight 2,760lb.

2000 Automatic, produced 1967, and 2000SC Automatic, produced 1968-73
As 2000/2000SC, except:
Transmission: Borg-Warner type 35 3-speed automatic transmission. Gear ratios 2.39:1, 1.45:1, 1:1, reverse 2.09:1. Top gear 19.2mph/1,000rpm.
Dimensions: Running weight 2,775lb.

2000TC, produced 1967-73
As 2000/2000SC, except:
Engine: 10:1 CR. Twin SU carburettors. 124bhp SAE at 5,500rpm; 109.5bhp DIN at 5,500rpm. Max torque 132lb/ft SAE at 4,000rpm; 124lb/ft DIN at 2,750rpm.
Steering, suspension and brakes: Wire wheels optional (1967-October 1969 approx).
Dimensions: Running weight 2,810lb.

2200SC, produced 1974-77
As 2000SC, except:
Engine: 4-cyl, 90.5mm x 85.7mm, 2,205cc OHC. 9:1CR. 5-bearing crankshaft, single SU carburettor. 98bhp DIN at 5,000rpm. Max torque 126lb/ft DIN at 2,500rpm.
Transmission: Top gear 19.7mph/1,000rpm.
Steering, suspension and brakes: Girling 10.36in front discs.
Dimensions: Length 179.31in. Height 55.25in. Ground clearance 6in. Running weight 2,822lb.

2200SC Automatic, produced 1974-77
As 2200SC, except:
Transmission: Borg-Warner type 35 3-speed and reverse automatic transmission. Gear ratios 2.39:1, 1.45:1, 1:1, reverse 2.09:1. Top gear 19.7mph/1,000rpm.
Dimensions: Running weight 2,855lb.

2200TC, produced 1974-77
As 2200SC, except:
Engine: Twin SU carburettors. 115bhp DIN at 5,000rpm. Max torque 135lb/ft DIN at 3,000rpm.
Dimensions: Length 180.56in. Running weight 2,829lb.

Three Thousand Five, produced 1968-70, and 3500, produced 1971-76
As 2000SC Automatic, except:
Engine: V8-cyl, 88.9mm x 71.1mm, 3,528cc OHV. 10.5:1 CR (1968-73); 9.25:1 CR (1974-76). 5-bearing crankshaft, twin SU carburettors. 184bhp SAE at 5,200rpm; 144bhp DIN at 5,000rpm (1968-73); 143bhp DIN at 5,000rpm (1974-76). Max torque 226lb/ft SAE at 3,000rpm; 197lb/ft DIN at 2,700rpm (1968-73); 202lb/ft DIN at 2,700rpm (1974-76).
Transmission: Borg-Warner type 65 3-speed automatic transmission (1974-76). Gear ratios 2.39:1, 1.45:1, 1:1, reverse 2.09:1. Axle ratio 3.08:1. Top gear 23.5mph/1,000rpm (1968-73); 24mph/1,000rpm (1974-76).
Steering, suspension and brakes: Burman recirculating-ball, worm-and-nut steering with variable ratio; power assistance optional. Servo-assisted Girling brakes, with 10.82in discs at front, 10.69in at rear. 185 HR-14 radial-ply tyres on 5.5in rims; Dunlop Denovo run-flat tyres on special wheels optionally available with power steering only (1974-76).
Dimensions: Rear track 51.75in. Length 179.75in. Height 55.75in. Ground clearance 7in. Running weight 2,862lb.

3500S, produced 1972-76
As 3500, except
Engine: 150bhp DIN at 5,000rpm (1972-73); 143bhp DIN at 5,000rpm (1974-76). Max torque 204lb/ft DIN at 2,700rpm (1972-73); 202lb/ft DIN at 2,700rpm (1974-76).
Transmission: 4-speed all-synchromesh gearbox with reverse. Gear ratios 3.62:1, 2.13:1, 1.39:1, 1:1, reverse 3.43:1.
Dimensions: Running weight 2,868lb.

APPENDIX B
Chassis number sequences and production figures

In the period covered by this book, the Rover Company used no fewer than seven different chassis numbering systems (the chassis number became known as the commission number on P5 and P6 chassisless models).

1934-1936 model-years
Six-digit numbers. There were no Export models as such and cars shipped to overseas markets were numbered within the main sequence.

First digit indicates model-year	Second digit indicates model
4 = 1934	0 = 10hp
5 = 1935	1 = 12hp
6 = 1936	2 = 14hp
	3 = Speed 14hp
	4 = 12hp long wheelbase

The last four digits indicate the serial number, commencing from 1001 in each series for each model-year.

1937-1939 model-years
Six-digit numbers, arranged as in 1934-1936, except that the second digit indicators differ in a number of instances to take account of new or changed models.

0 = 10hp Saloon
1 = 12hp Saloon
2 = 14hp Saloon
3 = 14hp Sports Saloon (and 1939 14hp Drophead Coupe)
4 = 12hp Sports Saloon
5 = 16hp Saloon (and 1937 16hp Sports Saloon)
6 = 16hp Sports Saloon (except 1937), 16hp Drophead Coupe and 1937 Speed Twenty Sports Saloon
7 = 20hp Sports Saloon (except 1937) and 20hp Drophead Coupe.

1940, 1946-1949 model-years
Seven-digit numbers, preceded on Export models for 1946-49 by an R or L prefix to denote right-hand or left-hand drive.

First digit indicates model-year	Second digit indicates model	Third digit indicates body type
0 = 1940	1 = 10hp	1 = Saloon
6 = 1946	2 = 12hp or 60	3 = Sports or 4-light Saloon
7 = 1947	3 = 14hp	4 = Drophead Coupe
8 = 1948	4 = 16hp or 75	5 = Tourer
9 = 1949		

The last four digits indicate the serial number, commencing from 0001 in each series for each model-year.

1950-1955 model-years
Eight-digit numbers, preceded on Export models for 1950 only by an R or L prefix to denote right-hand or left-hand drive.

First digit indicates model-year	Second digit indicates model
0 = 1950	3 = 60
1 = 1951	4 = 75
etc	5 = 90

Third digit indicates body type	Fourth digit (except 1950 models) indicates specification
3 = Saloon	
4 = CKD	0 = Home Market
	3 = LHD Export
	6 = RHD Export

The last four digits (five on 1950 models) indicate the serial number, commencing from 0001 (or 00001) in each series for each model-year.

1956 model-year
Nine-digit numbers.

First digit indicates type	Second digit indicates model
3 = Car (ie, as distinct from Land-Rover)	3 = 60
	4 = 75
	5 = 90

Third digit indicates specification	Fourth digit indicates model-year
0 = Home Market	6 = 1956
3 = LHD Export	
4 = LHD CKD Export	
6 = RHD Export	
7 = RHD CKD Export	

The last five digits indicate the serial number, commencing from 00001 in each series. Note: 16 1956-season 90 models were built and numbered before the introduction of the new system. These bore chassis numbers 65300001-65300016.

136

1957-1961 model-years

Nine-digit numbers. The first digit in all cases is 6, followed by a pair of digits in the sequence 00 to 54 indicating model and specification. See chassis number lists for full details; several number sequences were allocated but not actually issued. The fourth digit indicates the model-year (7 = 1957, etc) and the last five digits indicate the serial number, commencing from 00001 in each series for each model-year.

1962-1977 model-years

Eight-digit numbers, plus suffix letters. The first three digits, in the sequences 400 to 495 and 725 to 861, indicate the model and specification. See chassis number lists for full details; several number sequences were allocated but not actually issued. The last five digits indicate the serial number, commencing from 00001 in each series. The suffix letters indicate design modifications which are of importance in servicing the car. There is no digit to indicate the year or model-year of manufacture.

1937-1940, 1946-1947 model-years

Chassis commencing numbers

	10 Sal	10 Cpe	12 Sal	12 S.Sal	12 Tr	14 Sal	14 S.Sal	14 DHC	16 Sal	16 S.Sal	16 DHC	20 S.Sal	20 DHC
1937	701001	-	711001	711001	-	721001	721001	-	751001	751001	-	761001	-
1938	801001	881001	811001	841001	-	821001	831001	-	851001	861001	-	871001	-
1939	901001	981001	911001	941001	-	921001	931001	931001	951001	961001	961001	971001	971001
1940	0110001	0120001	0210001	0230001	-	0310001	0330001	0340001	0410001	0430001	0440001	0530001	0540001
1946	6110001	-	6210001	6230001	-	6310001	6330001	-	6410001	6430001	-	-	-
1947	7110001	-	7210001	7230001	7250001	7310001	7330001	-	7410001	7430001	-	-	-

Note: 1946-season cars were built between December 1945 and December 1946, 1947-season cars between January and December 1947.

Production totals

Note: As no prewar model-by-model records have survived, these production figures should be considered as estimates only.

	10S	10C	12S	12SS	12T	14S	14SS	14D	16S	16SS	16D	20SS	20D
1937	1,750	-	3,550*	3,550*	-	3,050*	3,050*	-	1,335*	1,335*	-	200	-
1938	1,500	250	2,800	800	-	2,000	900	-	1,500	550	-	300	-
1939	2,300	250	2,800	800	-	2,300	790*	790*	1,000	440*	440*	120*	120*
1940	1,188	25	831	205	-	428	118	12	185	88	11	18	3
1946	1,340	-	1,580	240	-	620	235	-	875	225	-	-	-
1947	1,300	-	2,300	520	200	700	150	-	2,325	725	-	-	-

* In six instances production figures duplicated in adjacent columns refer to the combined totals for the two models concerned.

P3 models

Chassis commencing numbers

	60 6-light	60 4-light	75 6-light	75 4-light	75 DHC
1948	8210001	8230001	8410001	8430001	8440001
1949	9210001	9230001	9410001	9430001	-

Note: 1948 season cars were built during the 1948 calendar year; 1949 season cars between January and August 1949.

Production totals

	60 6-light	60 4-light	75 6-light	75 4-light	75 DHC
1948	655	304	3,441	1,720	2
1949	256	59	1,755	919	-

1934-1936 model-years

Chassis commencing numbers

	10	12	12 LWB	12 SWB	14	Speed 14
1934	401001	411001	-	-	421001	431001
1935	501001	-	511001	541001	521001	531001
1936	601001	-	611001	641001	621001	631001

Production totals

Note: As no model-by-model records have survived, these production figures should be considered as estimates only.

	10	12	12 LWB	12 SWB	14	Speed 14
1934	2,200	1,230	-	-	2,000	150
1935	1,752	-	1,327	513	3,556	130
1936	1,750	-	1,955	750	3,908	100

P4 models
Chassis commencing numbers

	Model	Home Market	RHD Export	RHD CKD	LHD Export	LHD CKD
1950	75	04300001	R04300001	R04600001	L04300001	-
	-*	05300001	-	-	-	-
1951	75	14300001	14330001	14360001	1463001	-
1952	75	24300001	24330001	24360001	24630001	24660001
1953	75	34300001	34330001	34360001	34630001	34660001
1954	60	43300001	43330001	43360001	43630001	-
	75	44300001	44330001	44360001	44730001	-
	90	45300001	45330001	45360001	45830001	
1955	60	53300001	53330001	53360001	53630001	-
	75	54300001	54330001	54360001	54730001	-
	90	55300001	55330001	55360001	55830001	-
1956	60	330600001	333600001	334600001	336600001	-
	75	340600001	343600001	344600001	346600001	-
	90	65300001	-	-	-	-
	90	350600001	353600001	354600001	356600001	-
1957	60	600700001	601700001	602700001	603700001	-
	75	605700001	606700001	607700001	608700001	-
	90	610700001	611700001	612700001	613700001	-
	105R	615700001	616700001	-	618700001	-
	105S	620700001	621700001	-	623700001	-
1958	60	600800001	601800001	-	603800001	-
	75	605800001	606800001	-	608800001	-
	90	610800001	611800001	612800001	613800001	-
	105R	615800001	616800001	-	618800001	-
	105S	620800001	621800001	-	623800001	-
1959	60	600900001	601900001	602900001	603900001	-
	75	605900001	606900001	-	608900001	-
	90	610900001	611900001	612900001	613900001	-
	105	620900001	621900001	622900001	623900001	-
1960	80	645000001	646000001	647000001	648000001	-
	100	650000001	651000001	652000001	653000001	-
1961	80	645100001	646100001	647100001	648100001	-
	100	650100001	651100001	652100001	653100001	-
1961	80	74500001	74600001	74700001	74800001	-
-62	100	75000001	75100001	75200001	75300001	-
1963	95	76000001	76100001	-	76300001	-
-64	110	76500001	76600001	-	76800001	-

*Prototype 2.6-litre cars.

Production totals (see next page)

Note: These production figures are taken from the despatch records of the Rover Company, currently held by BL Heritage. They differ from earlier figures based on financial records published by Graham Robson and repeated by the present author in *The Postwar Rover: P4 and P5*. The present figures are based on model-year; the earlier published figures were based on financial year.

	Model	Home Market	RHD Export	RHD CKD	LHD Export	LHD CKD	Model total	Model-year total
1950	75	figures for sub-types not available					5,220†	
	(*)	30	-	-	-	-	30	5,250
1951	75	3,211	4,400	126	2,542	-	10,279†	10,279†
1952	75	1,927	997	54	2,718	72	5,768	5,768
1953	75	4,742	1,068	64	2,036	90	8,000	8,000
1954	60	2,042	63	44	32	-	2,181	
	75	2,783	524	16	677	-	4,000	
	90	4,163	2,090	32	1,020	-	7,305	13,486
1955	60	1,395	68	20	8	-	1,491	
	75	2,963	206	12	454	-	3,637	
	90	5,607	2,030	62	581	-	8,280	13,408
1956	60	1,424‡	97	15	65	-	1,601	
	75	2,186‡	194	6	354	-	2,740	
	90	6,497‡	1,920	32	321	-	8,770	13,111
1957	60	769	60	2	24	-	855	
	75	843	105	2	187	-	1,137	
	90	2,256	1,007	8	212	-	3,493	
	105R	1,700	121	-	81	-	1,902	
	105S	1,239	135	-	128	-	1,502	8,889
1958	60	984 (+790)	93	-	28	-	1,895	
	75	1,222	85	-	115	-	1,422	
	90	3,081	956	12	138	-	4,187	
	105R	981	410 (+117)	-	130	-	1,638	
	105S	1,476 (+1,581)	245 (+263)	-	148	-	3,713	12,855
1959	60	1,529	78	6	30	-	1,643	
	75	940	55	-	43	-	1,038	
	90	3,168	481	16	203	-	3,868	
	105	1,736	162	14	114	-	2,026	8,575
1960	80	2,792	222	15	56	-	3,085	
	100	6,251	851	45	558	-	7,705	10,790
1961	80	1,762	110	12	66	-	1,950	
	100	3,867	434	30	169	-	4,400	6,350
1962	80	810	33	-	22	-	865	
	100	3,872	349	6	189	-	4,416	5,281
1963	95	2,206	165	-	42	-	2,413	
	110	2,658	133	-	41	-	2,832	5,245
1964	95	1,091	168	-	8	-	1,267	
	110	1,690	76	-	22	-	1,788	3,055

Overall total 130.342

Model totals:

60	9,666
75	43,241
80	5,900
90	35,903
95	3,680
100	16,521
105R	3,540
105S	5,215
105	2,026
110	4,620

plus 30 2.6-litre prototypes (*)

† 15 1950-51 season chassis were delivered to Wilks, Mackie & Co for conversion to Marauders. All were home market models.

‡ 154 home market cars for 1956 were converted to 1957 specification.

1958 season: Despatch records are incomplete. Production figures quoted are taken from available records; the figure in brackets is a computed figure representing the missing records. The computation has been based on the overall total of 130,342 chassis drawn from financial records, which is believed to be correct.

P5 models
Commission numbers

		Home Market	Export RHD	CKD RHD	Export LHD
3-litre Saloon					
1959 Mk I	Manual	625900001	626900001	-	628900001
	Auto	630900001	631900001		633900001
1960 Mk I	Manual	625000001	626000001	-	628000001
	Auto	630000001	631000001		633000001
1961 Mk I	Manual	625100001	626100001	627100001	628100001
	Auto	630100001	631100001	-	633100001
1962 Mk IA	Manual	72500001	72600001	72700001	72800001
	Auto	73000001	73100001	-	73300001
1963 Mk II	Manual	77000001	77100001	77200001	77300001
-1966	Auto	77500001	77600001	77700001	77800001
1966 Mk III	Manual	79500001	79600001	-	79800001
-1967	Auto	80000001	80100001	-	80300001
3-litre Coupe					
1963 Mk II	Manual	73500001	73600001	-	73800001
-1966	Auto	74000001	74100001		74300001
1966 Mk III	Manual	80500001	80600001	-	80800001
-1967	Auto	81000001	81100001	-	81300001
2.4-litre Saloon					
1962 Mk IA	Manual	-	-	-	78800001
2.6-litre Saloon					
1962 Mk IA	Manual	-	75600001	-	75800001
1963 Mk II	Manual	-	78100001	-	78300001
-1966					
3.5/3½-litre Saloon					
1967-1973 Automatic		84000001	84100001	-	84300001
3.5/3½-litre Coupe					
1967-1973 Automatic		84500001	84600001	-	84800001

Production totals

	Model	Home RHD Manual	Home RHD Auto	Export RHD Manual	Export RHD Auto	Export RHD CKD Manual	Export RHD Auto	Export LHD Manual	Export LHD Auto	Total	Overall total	
1959	Saloon	1,584	768	305	158	-	-	186	159	3,160	3,160	
1960	Saloon	3,061	2,236	971	511	-	-	368	599	7,746	7,746	
1961	Saloon	1,661	1,532	376	391	6	-	212	166	4,344	4,344	(Mk I: 15,250)
1962	Saloon	1,612	2,245	190	382	306	-	399	529	5,663		
	2.4	-	-	-	-	-	-	25	-	25		
	2.6	-	-	1	-	-	-	24	-	25	5,713	(Mk IA: 5,713)
1963	Saloon	1,682	2,095	173	447	156	42	362	356	5,313		
	Coupe	237	180	15	18	-	-	58	38	546		
	2.6	-	-	6	-	-	-	43	-	49	5,908	
1964	Saloon	1,556	2,198	174	332	60	72	204	256	4,852		
	Coupe	951	1,250	29	92	-	-	161	83	2,566		
	2.6	-	-	-	-	-	-	27	-	27	7,445	
1965	Saloon	1,473	2,509	180	267	36	36	164	159	4,824		
	Coupe	722	1,198	20	79	-	-	85	41	2,145		
	2.6	-	-	8	-	-	-	22	-	30	6,999	
1966	Saloon	146	297	27	62	-	-	21	28	581		
(Mk II)	Coupe	46	142	3	17	-	-	8	9	225	806	(Mk II: 21,158)
(Mk III)	Saloon	576	1,558	38	101	-	-	98	136	2,507		
	Coupe	425	1,117	7	48	-	-	65	44	1,706	4,213	(1966 season: 5,019)

Year	Model	Home RHD Manual	Home RHD Auto	Export RHD Manual	Export RHD Auto	Export RHD CKD Manual	Export RHD Auto	Export LHD Manual	Export LHD Auto	Total	Overall total	
1967	Saloon	247	830	50	144	-	-	61	80	1,412		
	Coupe	132	520	6	81	-	-	22	34	795	2,207	(Mk III 6,420)
1968	Saloon	-	2,433	-	104	-	-	-	116	2,653		
(3.5)	Coupe	-	1,610	-	80	-	-	-	89	1,779	4,432	
1969	Saloon	-	2,390	-	214	-	-	-	118	2,722		
(3½)	Coupe	-	2,014	-	160	-	-	-	141	2,315	5,037	
1970	Saloon	-	1,756	-	191	-	-	-	120	2,067		
	Coupe	-	1,320	-	128	-	-	-	103	1,551	3,618	
1971	Saloon	-	1,737	-	60	-	-	-	36	1,833		
	Coupe	-	1,461	-	62	-	-	-	26	1,549	3,382	
1972	Saloon	-	1,290	-	70	-	-	-	26	1,386		
	Coupe	-	1,005	-	35	-	-	-	32	1,072	2,458	
1973	Saloon	-	735	-	84	-	-	-	21	840		
	Coupe	-	785	-	37	-	-	-	11	833	1,673	

Model totals: 2.4-litre: 25
2.6-litre: 131
3-litre: 48,385 (Saloon 40,402; Coupe 7,983)
3.5/3½-litre: 20,600 (Saloon 11,501; Coupe 9,099)

P6 models
Commission numbers

	Home Market	Export RHD	CKD RHD	Export LHD
2000 (1964-1970)				
SC	40000001	40100001	40200001	40300001
Automatic	40500001	40600001	40700001	40800001
S	41000001	-	-	41300001
TC	41500001	41600001	41700001	41800001
Auto Federal	-	-	-	85800001
TC Federal	-	-	-	85900001
2000 Mk II (1971-1973)				
SC	43600001	43700001	-	43900001
Automatic	44100001	44200001	44300001	44400001
TC	44600001	44700001	44800001	44900001
TC Federal	-	-	-	43500001
2200 (1974-1977)				
SC	47100001	47200001	-	47400001
Automatic	47600001	47700001	-	47900001
TC	49100001	49200001	-	49400001
TC (Italy)	-	-	-	86800001
SC (Nigeria)	-	-	-	86900001
Three Thousand Five (1968-1970)	42500001	42600001	42700001	42800001
3500S Automatic (1970-1971)	43000001	-	-	43300001
3500 Mk II (1971-1976)	45100001	45200001	45300001	45400001
3500S Manual (1972-1976)	48100001	48200001	48300001	48400001

Notes: 1. No records exist to confirm that any 430-series cars were built. However, sightings of such vehicles have been reported. They may possibly have been prototypes converted from 425-series cars.
2. The numbering system was changed in January 1975 when the 868 and 869-series cars were discontinued. New serial number ranges were then allocated to cater for all varieties of a given model (ie, SC, TC etc), and cars were numbered consecutively within these ranges while the type indicator number changed according to specification. 471/472/474-series cars began at 47100882, continuing from where the 471-series had stopped, but the other ranges started anew as follows:

451/452/453/454 at 45127000   481/482/483/484 at 48113000
476/477/479   at 47704000   491/492/494   at 49108000

In addition, 3500 VIP models built in 1976 were given 861-prefix numbers within the 451/452/453/454 sequence.

Production totals

No complete and accurate set of production figures for P6 models exists at the time of writing. Although BL Heritage do have the Rover Company's despatch records for P6 and P6B, these, unfortunately, do not provide a full picture because they contain no details of CKD cars prior to January 1975, and there is some suspicion that details of certain other series (eg, 430-series Automatic 3500S cars with right-hand drive) are missing. Rather than provide an incomplete and only partially accurate year-by-year breakdown of production figures, therefore, it seems sensible to give simply the available overall figures. The despatch records show the following:

2000 Mk I		2000 Mk II		2200	
SC	79,019	SC	14,179	SC	9,216
Auto	16,516	Auto	10,418	Auto	6,126
TC	50,768	TC	31,810	TC	16,368
S	15	TC Federal	238	TC (Italy)	560
Auto Federal	940			SC (Nigeria)	100
TC Federal	4,987				

Total 4-cylinder cars: 246,260

Three Thousand Five	22,290	3500S Auto	2,043
3500 Mk II	37,709	3500S Manual	17,015

Total 8-cylinder cars: 79,057

Total all models: 325,317

In addition, the following CKD cars were built:

2000 Mk I		2000 Mk II		Three Thousand	
SC	at least 1,985	Auto	at least 6	Five	at least 205
Auto	at least 246	TC	at least 30	3500S Manual	at least 838
TC	at least 432				

No estimated CKD figures are available for 3500 Mk II models built prior to January 1975. In addition, at least 7 3500S Automatics with right-hand drive are believed to have been built.

When added to the above totals, these figures give:
4-cylinder cars: at least 248,959   8-cylinder cars: at least 80,107

Total all models: at least 329,066

The figure of 327,208 displayed on the last-of-line P6 in December 1976 appears to have been hastily computed on the basis of despatch records. The discrepancy of 1,891 cars between this and the figure of 325,317 quoted above is exactly accounted for by the commission numbers which were allocated but not used.

APPENDIX C
How Fast? How economical? How heavy? Performance figures for Classic Rovers

1933-47 models*

	10hp Sports Saloon	12hp Saloon	14hp Saloon (1,577cc)	Speed 14hp Streamline Coupe	14hp Saloon (1,901cc)	16hp Saloon	Speed 20 Sports Saloon	60	75 4-light
P3 models									
Maximum speed (mph)	64.75	67.16	67.75	80.5	72	77.6	80.36	72	75
Acceleration (sec)									
0-50mph	21.4	22.2	–	17.0	22.2	16.2	14.0	–	18.2
0-60mph	–	–	31.0	25.0	41.3	–	–	–	29.4
Standing ¼-mile (sec)	–	–	24.0	21.8	–	23.0	22.5	–	–
Direct top gear (sec)									
10-30mph	15.6	15.6	–	–	15.7	12.8	10.0	13.5	10.9
20-40mph	15.4	15.8	–	–	16.7	13.0	–	–	11.9
30-50mph	18.2	18.2	–	–	21.4	13.6	10.4	–	13.1
Fuel consumption (mpg)	30 approx	28	21	22	22-24	19	20	30 approx	23-28
Weight (lb)	2,548	2,548	2,912	2,800	3,209	3,136	3,136	2,940	3,084
Original test published	*Autocar* May 25 1934	*Autocar* August 25 1933	*Motor* Sept 24 1935	*Motor* April 2 1935	*Autocar* August 19 1938	*Motor* June 7 1938	*Motor* June 15 1937	*(Rover Company figures)*	*Autocar* February 4 1949

*****Note:** Road-tests of the 1930s were not conducted to the same exacting standards as their modern equivalents. These figures should therefore be treated as a rough guide only.

P4 models

	60 (freewheel)	75 (2,103cc)	75 (2,230cc; freewheel)	80 (overdrive)	90 (freewheel; 3.9 axle)	90 (freewheel; 4.3 axle)	90 (overdrive)	95	100 (overdrive)	105R De Luxe	105S (overdrive)	110 (overdrive)
Mean maximum speed (mph)	77.25	82.0	85.5	85.8	83.5	80.9	91.4	94.0	92.3	93.9	95.0	100.0
Acceleration (sec)												
0-30mph	5.4	6.8	6.6	7.2	5.4	5.0	5.7	–	5.7	8.1	5.5	5.4
0-40mph	–	–	10.4	9.7	–	–	8.9	–	8.7	12.4	–	7.7
0-50mph	15.5	16.2	15.6	17.4	13.3	12.7	13.8	12.9	12.9	17.4	12.8	11.6
0-60mph	23.2	23.1	21.0	22.8	19.8	19.6	18.4	18.0	17.9	23.1	17.9	15.9
0-70mph	36.4	35.6	32.3	35.4	30.7	29.0	26.4	–	26.0	30.7	26.75	–
0-80mph	–	–	–	–	–	–	38.2	–	37.1	44.1	37.7	–
Standing ¼-mile (sec)	23.1	–	22.5	23.4	21.6	21.4	21.1	–	21.0	24.0	20.45	20.6
Direct top gear (sec)												
10-30mph	10.8	12.7	11.2	–	10.4	9.0	9.9	11.4	9.9	5.9*	9.5	8.9
20-40mph	11.1	12.7	12.3	11.5	10.4	9.2	9.6	11.34	9.9	7.8*	9.6	9.1
30-50mph	11.9	13.6	13.4	12.7	11.5	10.1	10.2	12.35	9.9	9.3*	9.7	9.4
40-60mph	14.6	–	15.2	14.7	13.6	12.0	11.3	14.25	12.3	10.7*	10.6	11.0
50-70mph	21.8	–	20.1	17.8	16.8	15.7	13.6	16.38	13.2	13.4*	14.5	–
60-80mph	–	–	–	–	–	–	18.4	–	17.7	21.0*	20.8	–
Overall fuel consumption (mpg)	28.7	–	23.8	19.8	22.3	20.7	21.2	–	19.5	20.1	18.5	18.4
Typical fuel consumption (mpg)	24-35	–	–	18-26	20-26	20-24	–	18-25	17-27	23.6	18-25	24.8
Kerb weight (lb)	3,024	3,198	3,192	3,304	3,196	3,196	3,248	3,287‡	3,444	3,472	3,444	3,416
Original test published	Autocar August 20 1954	Autocar July 14 1950	Motor January 26 1955	Autocar December 25 1959	Autocar March 26 1954	Autocar March 26 1954	Motor September 21 1955	(Rover Company figures)	Autocar August 12 1960	Motor February 13 1957	Autocar February 22 1957	Motor January 30 1963

‡ Running weight   * Figures taken in 'Drive' (ie, Intermediate gear) where possible.

P5 and P5B models

	3-Litre Mk I (overdrive)	3-Litre Mk IA (automatic)	3-Litre Mk II Saloon (overdrive)	3-Litre Mk II Saloon (automatic)	3-Litre Mk II Coupe (overdrive)	3-Litre Mk II Coupe (automatic)	3-Litre Mk III Saloon (automatic)	3-Litre Mk III Coupe (overdrive)	3.5-Litre Saloon	3.5-Litre Coupe
Mean maximum speed (mph)	96.4	93.6	108	102	108.7	102.4	101.2	107	108	110
Acceleration (sec)										
0-30mph	5.0	6.2	4.5	5.9	4.8	6.5	5.6	4.9	4.8	3.8
0-40mph	7.5	9.8	7.3	8.4	7.3	9.8	8.1	7.2	6.6	5.5
0-50mph	11.7	14.3	10.1	12.5	10.3	13.4	11.4	10.7	8.9	7.8
0-60mph	16.2	20.2	14.5	17.1	15.0	17.7	15.8	15.0	12.4	10.7
0-70mph	22.7	27.9	19.0	24.1	20.4	26.0	21.4	20.3	16.3	14.6
0-80mph	31.5	38.5	26.4	35.0	29.0	34.5	29.2	28.4	21.8	19.7
0-90mph	46.8	–	33.9	54.9	39.6	47.6	45.2	42.3	31.5	27.3
0-100mph	–	–	–	–	–	–	–	–	45.0	39.3
Standing ¼-mile (sec)	20.3	22.0	19.8	20.8	19.6	21.5	20.8	19.6	18.3	18.4

	3-Litre Mk I (overdrive)	3-Litre Mk IA (automatic)	3-Litre Mk II Saloon (overdrive)	3-Litre Mk II Saloon (automatic)	3-Litre Mk II Coupe (overdrive)	3-Litre Mk II Coupe (automatic)	3-Litre Mk III Saloon (automatic)	3-Litre Mk III Coupe (overdrive)	3.5-Litre Saloon	3.5-Litre Coupe
Direct top gear (sec)										
10-30mph	–	–	8.8	–	9.7	4.5*	–	9.1	–	2.9*
20-40mph	8.8	–	8.5	11.7	9.4	5.8*	5.0*	9.0	6.8	3.2*
30-50mph	9.2	–	9.2	11.7	9.7	6.9*	6.9*	9.3	7.6	4.5*
40-60mph	10.3	12.8	10.1	12.0	9.9	7.9*	8.6*	9.8	8.5	6.1*
50-70mph	12.4	15.5	10.8	13.2	11.1	12.6*	9.9*	10.8	9.6	7.2*
60-80mph	15.7	19.3	11.6	17.9	12.8	16.8*	16.0*	13.1	11.8	9.9*
70-90mph	–	35.6	13.4	30.6	17.4	21.6*	27.8*	19.4	15.5	14.2*
80-100mph	–	–	–	–	–	–	–	–	19.8	20.2*
Overall fuel consumption (mpg)	19.2	17.4	17.5	15.6	17.6	15.4	17.4	18.2	19.2	17.2
Typical fuel consumption (mpg)	16-24	16-25	22	14-20	16-22	19.15	20.9	16-23	20	22.6
Kerb weight (lb)	3,640	3,730	3,752	3,780	3,752	3,780	3,765	3,836	3,517	3,517
Original test published	*Autocar* August 21 1959	December 1 1961	*Motor* October 3 1962	*Autocar* November 13 1964	*Autocar* July 5 1963	*Motor* March 4 1964	*Motor* March 19 1966	*Autocar* May 6 1966	*Autocar* September 28 1967	*Motor* October 7 1967

*Figures taken using kickdown where possible.

P6 and P6B models

	2000 (pre-production car)	2000 TC	2000 Automatic	2000 SC Mk II	2000 TC Mk II	2200 SC	2200 SC Automatic	2200 TC	3500	3500 Mk II	3500 S
Mean maximum speed (mph)	104.0	108.4	94.0	98.3	105.0	100.8	101.0	108.3‡	117.0	112.0	122.0
Acceleration (sec)											
0-30mph	4.5	3.8	6.3	4.3	3.9	–	5.3	3.6	3.5	3.8	3.1
0-40mph	7.3	5.8	9.2	6.8	6.1	–	7.6	5.7	5.1	5.7	4.8
0-50mph	10.1	8.5	12.8	9.7	8.6	9.09	10.4	8.2	7.0	7.9	6.9
0-60mph	14.6	11.9	18.0	13.6	12.2	13.42	14.5	11.5	9.5	10.8	9.1
0-70mph	20.1	16.5	24.7	19.5	16.5	–	20.0	15.5	13.1	14.4	12.9
0-80mph	27.1	22.0	35.6	27.1	22.1	–	27.4	21.2	17.3	18.6	16.4
0-90mph	38.8	31.2	56.7	41.4	32.5	–	40.0	29.4	22.9	25.4	21.2
0-100mph	–	–	–	–	–	–	–	–	32.7	36.4	29.3
Standing ¼-mile (sec)	19.4	18.4	21.5	19.4	18.5	19.37	19.7	18.3	17.6	17.9	16.8
Direct top gear (sec)											
10-30mph	13.9	–	–	–	–	–	–	–	3.5*	–	10.1
20-40mph	12.7	11.3	8.9	12.3	11.8	10.55	–	10.0	3.7*	–	8.5
30-50mph	11.8	10.7	11.0	12.0	11.2	10.43	–	9.6	3.9*	–	8.1
40-60mph	12.6	10.6	14.3	13.2	11.2	11.02	–	9.3	5.1*	8.1	7.8
50-70mph	15.3	12.4	18.0	15.7	12.5	11.55	12.3	10.2	6.2*	8.8	8.3
60-80mph	17.7	15.1	22.3	18.9	15.0	–	14.4	11.6	8.5*		9.0
70-90mph	19.6	18.1	33.3	24.4	21.4	–	19.9	15.9	11.7*	14.1	10.4
80-100mph	–	–	–	–	–	–	–	–	15.5*	19.1	13.5
Overall fuel consumption (mpg)	23.0	22.3	21.8	22.6	22.4	–	20.5	20.4	17.5	18.0	20.1
Typical fuel consumption (mpg)	29.0	26.1	20-26	28.6	25.0	29.3	22.0	25.7	21.3	19.0	23.0
Kerb weight (lb)	2,772	2,800	2,890	2,772	2,946	2,822	2,867	2,845	2,912	2,979	2,979
Original test published	*Motor* October 9 1963	*Motor* October 1 1966	*Autocar* September 30 1966	*Motor* December 12 1970	*Autocar* March 18 1971	(Rover Company figures)	*Autocar* October 4 1973	*Motor* October 6 1973	*Motor* April 20 1968	*Autocar* October 15 1970	*Autocar* October 21 1971

* Figures taken in D1 range, using kickdown where possible.   ‡ Rover Company official figure.